Try Reading Again

Try Reading Again

Again

**How to Motivate and Teach
Older Beginners, Age 10 and Up**

DeAnna Horstmeier, Ph.D.

Woodbine House 2012

First edition

Library of Congress Cataloging-in-Publication Data

Horstmeier, DeAnna.
  Try reading again : how to motivate and teach older beginners, age 10 and up / by DeAnna Horstmeier. --
1st ed.
     p. cm.
  Includes bibliographical references and index.
  ISBN 978-1-60613-028-5
  1. Reading--Remedial teaching. I. Title.
  LB1050.5.H67 2012
  372.43--dc23

                                                                                            2012019518

10 9 8 7 6 5 4 3 2 1

To the Guys on North Street

Table of Contents

CD—Includes all contents of Appendices A and B; Additional Level Three Stories

Introduction

As a consultant, I visited a middle school to do an observation on a student with Down syndrome. In his American history class, he was writing on a paper while he industriously turned the pages of the textbook. I observed to the teacher that he seemed to be doing the work for the class.

"Oh, no! He doesn't read at all," she said. "He wants to be like the rest of the students so he pretends to read and do work."

I then asked if he was getting any reading instruction.

"Yes, I work with him alone on survival words like *poison* and *emergency* on flashcards."

"How does he do with the flashcards?" I asked.

"Well, he tries to memorize them, but he doesn't seem to remember all of them from one lesson to another. However, at least he tries. I have another student here who won't even try. He copies the words from the book, but he won't work with me on the survival words—and he gets angry if I push."

I couldn't help but think that the survival words didn't have much meaning for this teacher's two students. Words on signs are often shown with pictures for non-English speakers anyway. Also, if the first student could learn *emergency* as a sight word, he could probably learn the shorter sight words that are a part of beginning reading instruction.

The student with Down syndrome that I observed had developed habits to disguise his lack of literacy. Some students develop even more sophisticated ways of disguising their reading disabilities. In contrast, the other nonreading student in the class was frustrated and discouraged with his lack of progress and had become a behavior problem. Have you known students like this?

I consider basic reading an important survival skill, and it deserves much teaching time and energy—even for the teachers and parents of older students. The approach described in *Try Reading Again* is designed for these older students who have not been able to learn to read through regular classroom instruction.

Who should use *Try Reading Again?*

- Intermediate and secondary teachers
- Parents
- Reading tutors
- Volunteers who work with individual students in reading

Which students will profit from learning with *Try Reading Again?*

- Students of any age who have not been successful with beginning reading or have fewer than 100 sight words
- Visual learners, especially those with Down syndrome and autism
- Students who are older (third through twelfth grades) and want age-appropriate materials
- Students who show little interest in beginning reading
- English as a Second Language (ESL) beginning learners
- Students with mild learning disabilities (students with severe learning disabilities or severe dyslexia will probably need a more intensive phonics program such as the Wilson program or others based on the Orton-Gillingham program)
- Any student being taught by parent, tutor, or teacher who wishes to use one book that has details on language experience stories, phonemic awareness/phonics, and structured beginning readings

Try Reading Again: The Triangle Reading Approach

This book recommends a "triangle" approach to teaching reading to struggling beginners. That is, three strategies are used simultaneously in order to engage the student in learning, ensure that he is successful from the start, and help him build basic skills that will ensure his continuing success. The three components of the program can be represented like this:

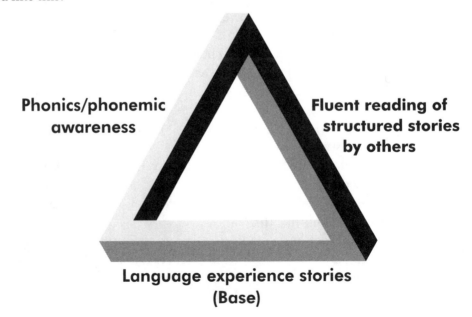

Phonics/phonemic awareness

Fluent reading of structured stories by others

Language experience stories (Base)

1. Language Experience Stories

Students who have not been successful with reading in the general classroom have a major barrier to further learning. Many times they are frustrated and would rather not try than risk failing again. ***Motivation*** must be addressed before other strategies can be successful. Researchers have found that students who read stories about their own experiences using their own vocabulary words are much more motivated to read (Pierson & Glaeser, 2003; Ashton-Warner, 1963, 1986). Creating stories about the student's own experiences in the student's own vocabulary is the base of the Triangle Approach.

2. Phonemic Awareness/Phonics

The second part of the Triangle Approach is ***phonemic awareness and phonics***. Some struggling older students have a reading vocabulary of more than 100 words, but they have difficulty figuring out new words because they do not have phonic patterns internalized. Most older beginning students come to instruction knowing the sounds of some of the consonants but need to learn the rest of the consonants, blends, digraphs, short and long vowel sounds, and simple prefixes and suffixes. Good readers usually intuit these concepts, but students with difficulties need to be specifically taught phonics and be shown how to use them when decoding.

Try Reading Again uses several strategies to help older beginners master phonics. First, age-appropriate phonics exercises are provided for the student. A simple-to-make game is also given for each major topic. The book also recommends the use of specific activities available on the free educational website *Starfall*. Most students who have Internet access will enjoy and benefit from the computer graphics and stories on *Starfall*. Phonics can be boring, so visiting the website really helps engagement and motivation. *Starfall* also has stories that illustrate the phonics principles that are being taught.

3. Structured Stories

Ultimately, students will need to read stories and content written by other authors. Older students are "turned off" by reading materials that are aimed at young children. Books such as *The Poky Little Puppy* (Lowery & Tennegren, 1942, 2001) and others with talking animals and preschool-type experiences can be embarrassing for intermediate or secondary level students to read and carry with their school books. ***Try Reading Again*** therefore includes structured stories with age-appropriate content and pictures. These stories are structured so that they gradually introduce sight words such as *it* and *was* that must be automatically read (and can't be guessed from pictures such as *cat* and *book)*. The Triangle Approach emphasizes both sight and content words in the structured stories. These ***age-appropriate stories*** teach ***vocabulary*** necessary for older students. The most commonly encountered sight words are taught in a sequenced order.

Each level of ***Try Reading Again*** has a language experiences section, a phonemic awareness-phonics section, and a section with age-appropriate, structured selections for new reading. The book has three levels of difficulty in each of the three basic areas—ending at a second- to third-grade reading level. If a student can finish the last level, he or she should be able to read some of the High Interest-Low Vocabulary books that are presently available from many publishers. Many other reading programs can be used at this point—for example, sight-based *Reading Milestones (1985, 2001),* or phonics-based *Reading Mastery (Englemann & Bruner, 1995)* or *Multiple Syllable Rewards* (Archer, Gleason, & Vacheon, 2006), etc.

Why Should You Use This Book?

- It combines language experience stories, phonemic awareness/phonics, and sequenced vocabulary stories.
- Clear procedures are listed for teaching reading.
- The stories and pictures are age appropriate for older students.
- The scope and sequence of reading instruction is contained in one book, rather than in separate phonics and reading books.
- The book has games and fun rhymes for every major topic in phonemic awareness and phonics.
- It introduces adult-type "nursery" rhymes to teach rhyming in phonemic awareness.
- It uses the website Starfall for computer-based activities, when appropriate.
- The book has mini-worksheets for student/teaching learning and independent worksheets for the student.
- Using examples, it teaches professionals and nonprofessionals how to write language experience stories, individualized to the student.
- It has objectives and evaluations for each topic in phonemic awareness/phonics. The different levels of difficulty can be used with Response to Intervention (RTI) Tiers II and III (secondary, more time-on-task intervention, and more intensive intervention). The evaluations at the end of each topic can be used for curriculum-based measurements that are an important part of RTI.
- And finally, you can use the instructional strategies and materials to make a meaningful difference in the life of someone who has been struggling to learn to read, as I've learned from personal experience.

The boy with Down syndrome in the above example was transferred to another school, where he finally did learn to read. I had another student who graduated from high school without being able to read. He didn't want to go to an adult education reading class. Instead, I tutored him weekly for a year (with the added incentive of feeding him lunch), using all three components of the Triangle Approach. He learned about 200 words and later felt comfortable finishing up with an adult education class.

His roommates were used to reading for him. I was there one day when they brought in a flyer for a bowling event. They started to read the flyer out loud, and he said, "Shut up, you guys. I can read it myself." He then proceeded to read the whole flyer—with pride.

Questions and Answers

Teaching Concerns

There are so many different ways to teach individuals to read. How do I know that the Triangle method described in this book is the best to teach my student?

There are a variety of programs for teaching reading. Most students can learn to read from any of the major reading programs. The older students targeted by the Triangle Approach have not been able to learn to read via the traditional methods used in their classrooms or tutoring. The approaches used have advantages for the slower learner. This approach is not totally whole language, phonemic awareness, or phonics (the most common approaches).

Language experience stories, in which students read about their own experiences as told in their words, are very helpful in giving struggling readers initial feelings of success. Once they have mastered reading their own words, they often become quite proficient in reading others' words by sight. However, there may be limits to the number of sight words they are able to memorize. Eventually, the students need to be able decode unfamiliar words by using the phonetic code. The problem is that some of the phonic programs available take a good deal of teaching time, use activities that are geared to younger children, or are dull. The Triangle Approach uses age appropriate, fun activities that can be taught in a school year.

Eventually, students must be able read selections written by various other authors. The Triangle approach supplies reading material that is appropriate for older students, rather than students in early childhood. Other resources are outlined that students can use once they reach first and second grade reading levels.

My student can read complex language experience stories, but he has a lot of trouble with beginning phonics.

It is possible that a student can master many sight words through learning to read words that are part of his own vocabulary and experience (Browder et al., 2006). Phonics may be more difficult for the student because he sees the whole word and not its different parts. It is very possible that a student will not be on the same level in phonics as in language experience stories or in reading new stories.

Some Suggestions: You may not need to work on phonics as often as you do the language experience stories. Emphasize the fun parts of the phonics exercises and the material from the computer program Starfall. You may need to try beginning phonemic awareness exercises to see if the student needs review on initial consonants or on hearing rhyming words. Use some activities with visual or tactile (touching) emphasis such as magnetic letters or pictures or writing letters (if the student does not have fine motor problems). Be positive and try to make the activities as much fun as possible.

My student seems to do better when other students are learning with him.

Some students do better when competing with another student or doing poems and songs with another person. Parents, you can use siblings to help motivate your child to learn, as long as this does not discourage his. Do not use large groups because each student needs to be actively involved in the learning, and the adult needs to quickly correct mistakes or clear up misunderstandings about concepts.

My student thinks that the camp song rhymes are silly and doesn't want to learn them.

Some students do not want to sing if other people can hear them. For self-conscious students, chanting the words of songs will produce the same effect—namely, helping them to master a rule or concept. Sometimes the teacher is reluctant to sing or chant the rhymes and the student senses this. You have to show enthusiasm to get your students to enjoy the rhymes. You can use other poems or camp songs that may be more appropriate for your learners. Some students have difficulty hearing the endings of words, which makes rhyming hard. If so, you can go ahead in the Phonics sections and return to the rhymes only when you can tell that the student is hearing the ends of words.

I am not sure whether to try the Starfall program with my older student.

Find out whether the student plays video games or watches cartoons on TV or at the movies. If he or she is into video games or cartoons, he or she will probably like the Starfall program. You can preview the levels and see if there are obvious "babyish" pictures or stories in them. Then you can kid about the "babyish" things before the student sees them and still use the Starfall program. I have found that many older students adapt to the Starfall program because it is graphic and on the computer.

How much should I modify what the student says in making the language experience stories?

You need to use as many of the student's words as possible, including slang or words that are not so socially acceptable. However, be aware that students often speak in run-on sentences that are not ideal for learning reading. Repeat the words of the run-on sentence in a simple sentence, saying "Do you mean . . . .?"

You may have to prompt the student with questions to finish the whole story. A prompt such as "What did you do after you got home?" may help the student learn how to tell a story. The story should not be very long, depending on the student's attention span. It is better to write two stories about the same event than to write an extremely long story. If you can prompt a little humor in the story, it will make the story more interesting. For example, one of my students made the comment, "Of course, I am perfect." It was easy to prompt him to say, "Of course, I am perfect" after each small event, and he laughed every time he read it.

Doesn't the student get bored reading the same language experience story or other stories over and over?

Repetition is very important in the Triangle Approach. You should tell the students that you are not just reading to get the content of the story (to find out what happens). When **learning** to read, students need to read stories over and over so that they "over learn" the words and can read the story fluently. When you read science and social studies textbooks, you can read to understand what is said, but in **learning** reading you have to almost memorize the story in order to read it fluently. Many children learn to read by memorizing favorite stories due to frequent readings. The National Reading Panel (NICHD, 2000) found that repeated oral reading with feedback resulted in significant reading improvement.

What if this book does not have enough stories and exercises to teach my student the various principles of reading?

Some Suggestions: Look at the resource section in this book for other materials on the needed principle or reading level. Most books available on lower reading levels begin at the second or third grade level. Even library books may introduce words too quickly for the beginning reader. Easier reading materials, however, are listed in the resource section.

If your student has a compelling interest, use that to make stories. Get some pictures of the specific interest (e.g., trains) and write a story with trains as the main characters. You will know how to write stories that are appropriate for the student because of your experience writing the student's language experience stories. In this case, however, you will use *your* words to teach the principle or provide more practice reading at the grade level the student needs to work on.

For example:

Objective: to give practice in forming plural and -ing endings.

Nathan and his father were **coming** home from a ball game. They were **looking** for a train station. There ahead of them was the Metro train station. Nathan saw three trains **coming** into the station. Two trains were **pulling** coal cars. People were **riding** in a passenger train. Nathan and his father ran to the passenger train. It was good to be **riding** instead of **walking**.

Another strategy is to find teenage magazines and rewrite the content so it is suitable for your student. Use Post-It notes with the simplified content pasted over the regular text.

For example, you could paste the following under a picture of the actor John Stamos:

John Stamos was on the TV show *Full House* for eight years.

Now he plays a doctor on the TV show *ER*, a show about hospitals.

You may also have the student read popular song lyrics. (Preview them first.) These often have rhymes and are usually very interesting to older students. Songs may use more of the right brain by adding imagery, enhancing the student's learning.

Finally, you may want to look into buying some books from a commercially available high/low reading series. You can usually find some sample stories on the websites for these reading series. You can also find a few programs such as A to Z Reading that have reading material available for a fee. See the resource section of this book.

What about students with disabilities that make speech difficult or impossible?

First, you should recognize that understanding sign language is a form of reading. So, if you have a student who uses signs, have him sign the words on the page.

If the student has little speech and does not sign, he can indicate that he understands the meaning of a word by pointing. Have the student point to a named word before turning the page (or having the page turned for him). Another way to check that he can read the words is to deliberately read one word in a sentence wrong and ask him to point to it. To help a student with fine motor problems turn the page, put your finger in the next page or put in a page fluffer (a piece of sponge that separates the pages so the student can turn them more easily).

For a student with almost no speech, an adult can program a switch to say a phrase that is used frequently in the story, and the student can push the switch at the appropriate time. The student should be looking at the words in the story so he knows when to push the switch. You may also be able to get recorder apps for your smart phone or tablet computer and record the phrase for the student that way.

Computers or augmentative communication devices can help many students with physical disabilities. The printing can be made larger, the device can highlight or pronounce the word, keys can be made more accessible, and symbols or pictures can be added to help the student learn.

Smart phones and tablet computers (such as iPads) will probably be sources of learning games and reading programs that may have application for readers with physical disabilities. See the resource section for suggestions of possible apps.

Educational Concerns

How does the Triangle Approach address the five major areas in learning to read as described by the National Reading Panel? (National Institute of Child Health and Human Development, 2000)?

The Triangle approach addresses the five areas:

1. **Phonemic Awareness** – identifying letter sounds, hearing initial consonants, rhyming words
2. **Alphabetic Principle** (phonics) – letter knowledge, consonants, short vowels, long vowels, blends, word endings, r-controlled vowels, multisyllabic words
3. **Vocabulary** – learning to read the student's own words and sequenced learning of other words. Individual words are written on cards, and the student names the words as he picks up the cards. Any cards the student does not name correctly are located in the actual language story and correctly read.
4. **Fluency**—repeated oral readings of language experience stories and other structured stories.
5. **Comprehension** – the student understands his own stories, is asked questions following other authors' stories, and develops good phonics understanding so attention can be given to meaning of content.

My principal says that we have to have research-based programs to teach reading. Is the Triangle Approach used in Try Reading Again researched?

The entire Triangle Approach has not been tested with a large number of students and control groups. However, the approaches used in the Triangle Approach have been researched separately.

The language experience approach has been used extensively in schools (Hall, 1978; Heffner, 2004). Many research studies were done comparing the reading of students taught by basal reading series versus the language experience approach (Hall, 1978). Most of the studies showed that the children being taught with the language experience approach were reading as well as (or better) than the children taught with the basal series (Hildreth, 1995, Kenrick, 1966; Stauffer, Vilscek, Morgan, & Cleland, 1966, and others, as cited in Hall, 1978). The language experience approach has also been successfully used using digital photography and computers with young children (Labbo, Eakle, & Montero, 2002), at the secondary level, and for students learning English as a second language.

The National Reading Panel, in a survey of over 100,000 research studies on reading, concluded that "effective reading instruction includes teaching children to break apart and manipulate the sounds in words (phonemic awareness), teaching them that these sounds are represented by letters of the alphabet which can then be blended together to form words (phonics)" (National Institute of Health, 2000). Reid Lyons and the other members of the Reading Panel concluded that: "Disabled readers must be presented highly structured, explicit and intensive instruction in phonics" (L. Sherman, 2000).

However, Lyons also said, "No matter how bright the child or how interesting the reading material, a child will not learn to read unless he or she understands how print is translated into sound. Likewise, no matter how much phonological awareness and phonics knowledge a youngster has, the child will not want to engage in reading and writing unless it is meaningful and interesting and taught in an exciting and vibrant fashion" (L. Sherman, 2000).

The Triangle Approach includes a phonemic awareness/phonics section with games, poems, and exercises. In addition, the Triangle Approach has a structured story section that includes sequenced vocabulary and age-appropriate content that is interesting and meaningful.

Students who have not learned to read after several years of instruction in the general classroom need to have more intensive instruction and perhaps a different approach. The Triangle Approach covers decoding skills, interest-based language experience stories, and structured, sequenced vocabulary stories; so possibly one of those approaches would apply to your older student.

My school is using Response to Intervention (RTI) for reading instruction. How does the Triangle Approach fit into RTI?

The major purpose for RTI is to catch students who are falling behind in reading before they have experienced real failure with its accompanying discouragement and frustration. Giving more intervention earlier and taking frequent data should help most students show improvement in reading skills. Most students who need RTI will get general reading classroom instruction (level one). Those who fall behind get more intense instruction in level two. Only students who do not respond to level two instructions get specialized, more intense reading intervention.

The Triangle Approach is intended to help students who have not learned in regular classroom instruction. For example, the student's responses to level two intervention may indicate that he needs phonics training. The Triangle Approach has phonics training designed for the older student that can be used. However, much of the material in the Triangle Approach will be most useful for students at level three. The primary users will be those who can work with one to three students, including teachers, parents, tutors, and volunteers. Small assessments are given regularly so that the data can be used to gauge the student's response to intervention.

Approaches to Teaching Reading
Research and Controversies

Reading Problems

According to the report *Early Warning! Why Reading by the End of Third Grade Matters* from the Annie E. Casey Foundation (2010), 68 percent of all fourth grade public school students in the United States are struggling readers. This is the percentage of fourth graders who did not score "proficient" in 2009 on reading tests administered through the National Assessment of Educational Progress, a testing program mandated by the U.S. Congress.

Of that 68 percent, a significant number are not able to read the letters of the alphabet or read over 50 words independently. They are essentially nonreaders. Unfortunately, most instruction in learning to read is concentrated in kindergarten through third grade. By fourth grade, students are expected to use reading skills to learn content in other subjects.

Sadly, many struggling readers do not ever "catch up" with their peers who can read on grade level. Although it is possible to teach reading skills at any time in a student's school career or in adult classes, not much reading instruction is done in schools at the intermediate or secondary levels. Why?

- Students have had experiences of failure and are frustrated. As a result, they often do not want to try to read, and develop behaviors to avoid reading.
- There is a lack of age-appropriate materials for older students.
- Those who set the curricula for school systems have the perception that time is not available for teaching the skill of reading in the upper grades.
- Teachers of older students may feel that they lack expertise in teaching reading.

There are a variety of reasons why students reach the fourth grade without achieving proficiency in reading. Some of them have significant developmental disabilities that have a pervasive effect on many areas of learning, not just reading. Others have a learning disability that makes reading a struggle for them. Still others are not taught in the way that they can readily learn—for example, they are visual learners, but receive most of their instruction through lectures. Other students find reading instruction boring when the content is foreign to their interests.

As mentioned in the Introduction, students who have the most severe reading disabilities are often best served when they are instructed systematically in reading methods developed specifically for students with dyslexia (for example, the *Wilson Reading System* (2004, 2010), J. F. Greene's *Language!* (2000), or G. Johnson's and S. Engelmann's *Corrective Reading* (1999).

For older struggling readers, however, there is no consensus as to the best teaching approach. Most of the research on teaching reading to students with learning disabilities has focused on phonemic awareness and phonics. People with developmental disabilities, on the other hand, often receive reading instruction focused on learning sight words (Browder, Wakeman, Sponner, Ahlgrim-Delzell, & Algozzine, 2006). Neither of these approaches is inherently "wrong" for a given student. They are only wrong: 1) if the student is not successful in learning to read proficiently using that approach, and 2) if the student has become discouraged about learning to read. (There has been little research on motivation of older, discouraged reading students.)

In the sections below, I will explain the rationale for combining different teaching approaches in order to help these older, struggling individuals learn to read.

Language Experience Stories

In 1963, Sylvia Ashton-Warner published a book called *Teacher* which described how the Maori children in New Zealand were not learning to read with the basic series used by other students because the stories were not about their culture and did not incorporate the words they actually used. She hit upon the idea of writing stories using her Maori students' own words. This motivated them to learn to read. After publication of Ashton-Warner's book, many schools started using her approach for beginning reading. A prominent educator, Rob Stauffer, wrote a book called *The Language Experience Approach to the Teaching of Reading* (1970) which was widely used.

Ashton-Warner's and Stauffer's approach to teaching reading is now known as the language experience approach (LEA). It draws on real-life experiences of students so that their reading materials are in their own language and about content that is important to them. To make reading materials, the student is prompted to talk about an event that is important to him. The teacher writes down the student's words and then uses that text for beginning reading instruction.

In the 1960s and '70s, many research studies compared the reading abilities of students taught with basal reading series versus those taught with the language experience approach. Most of the studies showed that the children who were taught with the language experience approach read as well as (or better) than the children taught with the basal series (Kenrick, 1966; Stauffer, 1966; Vilscek, Morgan, & Cleland, 1966, and others as cited in Hall, 1981).

In the late 1980s and '90s, Ken Goodman, Frank Smith, Marie Clay, and others picked up the language experience approach as part of the whole language movement. They felt that students learned to read better through experience and exposure than through analysis and skill instruction. (The whole language approach focuses on teaching reading, writing, and language together as a "whole." It also focuses on much reading of good literature, with independent silent reading as a major component. Phonics learning is addressed only when it comes up in the course of reading, and there is a lack of sequenced vocabulary.)

For a time, discussion in the reading literature focused on the phonics (plus phonemic-awareness) approach versus the whole language approach. The language experience approach was somewhat neglected, in spite of its good results in fluency, vocabulary, comprehension, and motivation.

More recently, there has been a mild resurgence of interest in the language experience approach. It has been used at the secondary level, and has been used successfully with adults and students learning English as a second language (Gambell & Sajtos, 2001; Taylor, 1992; Pierson & Glaeser, 2003). According to two of these researchers, "The research clearly demonstrates the advantages to teaching the Language Experience Approach… (because) children are motivated to want to read" (Pierson and Glaeser, 2003).

Currently, several websites for parents discuss how to use the language experience approach in teaching reading at home:

- www.literacyconnections.com/InTheirOwnWords.php
- www.succeedtoread.com/makeabook.html
- www.readingmethod.com/language-experience.html
- www.suite101.com/content/language-experience-approach-at-home

Try Reading Again uses language experience stories for older students who have had difficulty with beginning reading because it uses the student's own content, thus supplying motivation, and also produces the positive effects demonstrated through research.

Phonemic Awareness/Phonics

In 1997, the National Reading Panel was formed at the request of the U.S. Congress with the goal of assessing the effectiveness of different approaches used to teach children to read. In 2000, this panel conducted a comprehensive analysis of the research in reading. The following year, President George W. Bush announced that the NRP's report would be the basis of federal literacy policy. The International Reading Organization summarized the report by stating that the focus of beginning readers needed to be on the five big ideas in reading:

1. Phonemic-awareness (teaching children to break apart, blend, and manipulate the sounds in words)
2. Phonics (teaching that these sounds are represented by letters)
3. Fluency in oral reading of text
4. Vocabulary (words and their meanings)
5. Comprehension (providing comprehension strategies to get meaning)

Most of the programs funded by Reading First, the government's reading intervention, focused a great deal on the first two elements of phonemic awareness and phonics, as well as the other elements. This focus on phonics undoubtedly helped many beginning and struggling readers to learn to read. There seems to be some agreement among reading experts (Lyon, 1999; Moats, 1999; Shaywitz, 1992; and Torgesen, 1998) that, when beginning readers are really struggling, introducing phonemic awareness and phonics is the most effective method to "jump start" emergent reading. Most students can learn some sight words by memory. However, there are limits to memory. At some point, students need to learn a system of relating the written letters to the sounds of words—phonics.

Recent research has also focused attention on the value of phonemic awareness. Phonemic awareness does not involve written letters. It is only about recognizing the sounds that make up spoken words and being able to manipulate those sounds. Researchers have found that the earliest indication of possible reading difficulties is lack of phonemic awareness. If a child can't hear the individual sounds in a word, he or she won't be able to make the leap of linking those sounds to letters (Sherman, 2000). The Triangle Approach to reading contains both phonemic awareness and phonics lessons. Although these types of activities have been described as boring, but very useful, the Triangle Approach involves games, worksheets, adult "nursery rhymes," and use of the website Starfall (when appropriate)—all of which can make the learning enjoyable when used by an enthusiastic teacher. Many of the lessons in phonemic awareness are combined with phonics work (letters), since older students usually are well acquainted with letters and frequently profit from the visual stimulus of written material. The phonemic awareness/phonics lessons are only a part of the Triangle program, with the other elements of reading such as vocabulary, fluency, and comprehension addressed in the Language Experience and Structured Stories sections.

Combined Approaches

Having used the phonemic awareness/phonics approach during the late '90s and early 2000s, schools in America are aware of the benefits of the approach. But now they are also willing to admit what many teachers and parents recognized long ago—that "all phonics all the time" doesn't work for all children.

In fact, members of the National Reading Panel had already reached that conclusion. G. Reid Lyon (2002), the former Chief of the Child Development and Behavior Branch within the National Institute of Child Health and Human Development (NICHD), summed up the conclusion of the researchers: "Without a doubt, we have found that teaching methods that are based upon one philosophy, such as 'the whole-language approach' or 'the phonics method' are counterproductive for children with reading disabilities. No matter how bright the child and how interesting the reading material, a child will not learn to read unless he or she understands how print is translated into language. Likewise, no matter how much phonological awareness and phonics knowledge a youngster has, the child will not want to engage in reading and writing unless it is meaningful and interesting and taught in an exciting and vibrant fashion" (Lyon, 2002).

Try Reading Again presents a combination of philosophies for struggling students—because researchers have acknowledged that that's what these students need, but also because my personal experience working with struggling readers has shown that this is the case.

Age-appropriate Structured Stories

Even when students have learned to decode regular words through phonics, there are many words that are not regular (called "outlaws" in the Triangle Approach) that need to be learned by sight. A list of many irregular words, as well as words that a reader needs to know automatically, is found in Appendix A3. These words are among the most frequently used (e.g., *the, and, does, said, you,* etc.) and are best learned in sentences that have meaning. In *Try Reading Again,* these words are introduced in the structured stories in Part 3. These stories are on themes designed to appeal to older children and adults, rather than on the more simplistic themes usually found in beginning reading books. They are mostly adaptations of true experiences (except for the legends and imaginary stories).

Vocabulary words are introduced in small steps and increase in difficulty as the students progress through the structured stories. This approach also gives the student frequent success, which is an important factor in motivating older children and adults to read. The goal is for the student to be able to read at a 2.5 or 3rd grade level so he can eventually use more conventional reading programs and regular classroom academic materials. Therefore, the student needs to learn the vocabulary and comprehension strategies that his peers are using.

An important part of the Triangle approach is having students repeatedly read the language experience and structured stories. This step is aimed at increased fluency, an important factor in the National Reading Panel's list of reading principles. If you need to measure the student's growth in oral reading fluency, you can test him or her with the Dynamic Indicators of Basic Early Literary Skills (DIBELS), which can be obtained for free from their website (produced by the University of Oregon).

Of course, comprehension or meaning is an important part of reading stories—and is easier for a student to grasp a story's meaning when it comes from the student's own experiences. Eventually, however, students have to be able to get meaning from other people's words, so the structured stories are necessary. When a student is struggling to decode words, he cannot concentrate on the meaning as well. The teacher, tutor, or parent needs to discuss meaning with the student at the appropriate level considering his command of phonics and decoding.

Principles of Teaching with the Triangle Reading Approach

1. **Repetition:** You need to establish at the beginning that part of learning to read is repetition. Your student will need to practice reading his own language experience stories and the structured stories until he can read them fluently. Frequent repetitions of the rhymes, flashcards, and other features of the phonemic awareness-phonics sections are also essential. When young children are learning to read, they often want to hear stories many, many times. We are reproducing that effect for the older students. Research has also shown that repeated readings are very effective in increasing fluency in oral reading. Fluency skills include accuracy, speed, phrasing, intonation, and stress.

   Older students may not want to read things over and over since students in the upper grades usually read only once for content. However, they must be taught that this repetition is an important part of learning to read. Each lesson should be started with a review of a previously learned concept. Practice needs to be part of learning for older students who have not progressed with the regular classroom reading program.

2. **Success:** Older students often are frustrated with their previous lack of success in reading. You, the teacher, may have to break down some of the steps in the lesson so

that students will have success quickly. Preteaching new vocabulary words can turn into a successful experience. You will also have to praise frequently, be positive, and cultivate an atmosphere of rapport with your student(s).

3. **Structure:** Older, discouraged students often respond to a structured routine of predictable lessons. They may feel more confident when they know exactly what to expect. It is usually easier for the teacher to make sure that he or she follows the proper scope and sequence of learning to read when the structure is in place. Most lessons should include a mixture of phonemic awareness/phonics activities and story reading each time. At first the language experience stories should be read over and over. When the student is reading the experience stories fluently, the structured stories by other writers should be introduced and read orally until fluent.

4. **Enthusiasm:** The student's success depends a lot on the teacher showing enthusiasm for the reading activities. Older students are much attuned to the teacher's feelings, and will pick up on the teacher's enthusiasm (or lack thereof). The Triangle Approach has interesting activities and games that can be fun for both teacher and student. The games are particularly important because they provide practice in a fun way. Don't reserve the games just for occasions when you think you have enough time in the lesson! The games give important practice for learning, and sometimes the students will play them even when it is not time for reading.

5. **Activity:** Involve the student in as much of the activity as possible. Pace the lessons so there is little down time. You can add activities to any of the lessons. The more the student is involved, the more he will learn—and the more opportunities you will have to determine whether he understands the concept or not. Teachers can find additional structured stories on the CD and other activities on the Starfall website under the Educators section. You will need to screen the Starfall activities for age-appropriateness. Use a small blackboard or whiteboard for both teacher's and student's writing and to keep the student actively involved.

6. **Generalization:** It is very important that students look in their language experience stories for examples of the principles they are learning. For example, if your student is learning about plurals, help him look for plural nouns in his stories. He also should apply the principles he is learning to new words that he encounters in the structured stories written by others. If there are no relevant examples in the stories, you should write some sample sentences for him (examples are given in the book). Learning phonemic awareness and phonics principles is of no use if the student does not use these skills when confronted with a word to be decoded in regular reading.

Triangle Reading Informal Assessment

Before using the Triangle Approach described in this book with your student(s), it is important to informally assess their reading skills. This will enable you to start them at the appropriate level in the Phonemic Awareness/Phonics activities. You will also gain important information about your student's abilities that can guide you in writing language experience stories that are at the right level of complexity for the student.

To start with, every student should be assessed on letter knowledge. You need to know what letters of the alphabet she knows. If you continue with the Triangle Reading Assessment, you will assess the student on all three elements of the Triangle approach to reading:

1. Testing phonics/phonemic awareness by assessing letter knowledge
2. Doing a short language experience story in the student's own words
3. Reading another person's appropriate story fluently

In testing letter knowledge, you can keep data on how many letters the student can name without hesitation. If the student passes Letter Knowledge, you can skip to Level One, Phonemic Awareness/Phonics. You have to use your own judgment as to whether the student is able to dictate a language experience story and learn to read it. Most teachers start students at Level One, Language Experiences. If, however, the student is able to read the starter story and other language experience stories easily, you may advance her to Level Two Language Experience Stories and begin having her read stories from Level One, Structured Reading (other people's stories).

1. Phonics/Phonemic Awareness (Letter Knowledge)

Objective: The student will be able to *name* the letters of the alphabet (upper and lower case).

Many students who have been trying to learn to read can identify some or all of the letters of the alphabet. It is not necessary to know the names of all the letters of the alphabet to be able to read. However, research has shown that students learning to read should be able to discriminate the letters from each other (Abededarian Reading Assessment, 2002). Knowing the names of the letters helps the student distinguish the letters from one another and also helps her understand what the teacher is trying to convey.

You don't have to teach students to identify letters that they already know. You also do not have to halt further reading instruction until a student can identify all the letters. Although students should eventually be able to name all the letters given in the assessment, you can progress with reading instruction while teaching the additional letter identifications that your students don't know. That is, you can combine instruction in letter identification with beginning reading instruction.

Letter Assessment

When the teacher points to the following letters, the student names or identifies them. If the student is not verbal, she can just point to the correct letter when the teacher names it; however, eventually you will want the student to be able to name the letters.

T	r	y	X	L	e	J	V	I	m
Q	B	w	P	s	g	N	d	C	a
F	b	E	O	H	A	z	q	l	M	n
J	i	f	D	R	G	h	k	t	U	j

The letters that are similar in the lower and the uppercase are given only one time. For example, uppercase /U/ is similar to lowercase /u/, so only uppercase /U/ is given in the assessment.

The student should be able to name each letter without struggle or long hesitation. This naming should be automatic before the letter is considered mastered.

Mark each letter which the student has named correctly. Of course, you will teach the letters incorrectly named as you teach beginning reading.

Evaluation:

- If the student can name 38 of the letters, she can be placed at Level One, Phonemic Awareness/Phonics.
- If the student names fewer than 38 of the letters, place her at the Preliminary level, Phonemic Awareness/Phonics for instruction in letter names.

2. Language Experience Stories

Since increasing motivation is one of the keys to the reading approach outlined in this book, it is essential that the student experience success early and often. Consequently, you need to make sure that she is successful in reading the first language experience stories you show her. I recommend that you introduce language experience stories by telling and writing your own story first so you can control the simplicity of the story.

Start the beginning reading procedure by telling the student about an experience that you have had. Make your story very simple, with short words. It should be three to four simple sentences long. Write the story down as the student watches. For example:

Teacher Story: Teacher: "Guess what happened to me?"

I got a flat tire.

I got a flat tire on my car.

I called AAA.

They fixed the flat tire.

1. After you tell the student your short experience, tell her you are going to write it down.
2. Print each of your sentences on the bottom of a separate piece of paper, putting some extra space between each word.
3. Draw one or two pictures that help identify the words, such as a tire or a car (in the sample below). Tell the student what your drawings depict, just in case you are not the best artist in the world. Your drawings do not have to be recognizable.

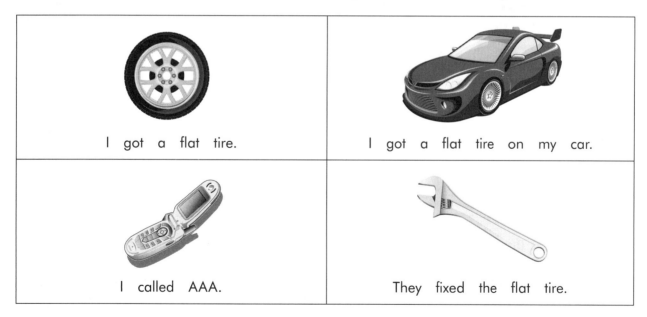

4. Read your story to the student, pointing to each word as you read.
5. Ask the student if she can read any of those words. Point to the words illustrated by your drawings, if she needs assistance.
6. Read your story again and ask her to read along on any words that she knows. Praise any words she says correctly.

Student Story:

1. Ask the student if she has an experience or story to tell. If you know some incident or a short experience the student has had at school or at home, you may want to prompt the student to tell that story.

2. If she only says long sentences or her words are not understandable, you can say, "You meant . . .?" (and shorten or fix the sentence). If she agrees that is what she meant or repeats your sentence, you can write down those words. We hope to be able to write down mostly the student's own words, but she may need some modeling when learning.

   Teacher: "Tell me about your lunch."
   Student: "I eat pizza."
   Teacher: "and . . . ?"
   Student: "I eat pizza and milk.
         It is good.
             I like pizza."

3. Draw a picture of a pizza and a glass of milk. You may want to put "mmm" near the word *good,* if the student uses that sound and gesture. If not, a happy face might work as an illustration.

4. Read the story to the student, pointing to each word as you read.

5. Then have the student read the story along with you.

6. Ask the student if she can read any of those words. Point to the words illustrated by your drawings, if she needs assistance.

7. Read the story together.

8. Write the words from the story in lower case (except for the word I) with marker on index cards. Remember that these words must be the ***student's own,*** not the words of the sample.

I	like	pizza	is
and	milk	it	good

9. Put the index cards on a table or the floor where the student can see them.

10. Have the student pick up any of the cards that she can read.

11. Match the incorrect or missed words on index cards with the same words in the story. Then let the student try again to read the words on the index cards.

Evaluation:

- If the student learned to read most of her own words (75 - 80%), go on to doing Level One, Language Experience Stories.
- If she does not know 75% of the words, make a simpler story and try again.

3. Structured Stories by Other Authors

The goal of teaching any student to read is for her to be able read material written by other people. Although some students starting out with the Triangle Approach may not be able to read other people's stories yet, you should assess your student on this skill now because there is a possibility she can read well enough to start with the structured stories at the same time as the language experience stories. (For most students, you will not start with structured stories until they are reading Level One language experience stories fluently.)

When using the Triangle Approach, students are introduced to structured stories written at a reading level that is easy for them—easier than the student written language experience stories. This material needs to be age-appropriate and interesting to the student. This helps ensure that the student is successful and continues to be motivated to learn to read. Repeated readings should help the student to read these stories fluently.

Simple Story:

1. Let the student look at the story "The Beach" (below). Ask her about the pictures. Does she know where the story takes place? Point out the word *beach.* Point out the other content words: *splash, water,* and *fun,* and explain their meanings if the student is not familiar with them.
2. Read the story to the student, pointing out the words. Read the story with the student.
3. Have the student read the story, with the teacher filling in any words not known.

The Beach

We walk in sand.

We splash in water.

We have fun.

Sight Words	Content Words
we	splash
in	water
	sand
the	fun
walk	beach
have	

4. Write the words on index cards and let the student pick the words she knows.

we	walk	in	splash
water	the	have	fun
beach	sand		

Evaluation:

- If the student learns three content words and three sight words and reads the story fluently (with appropriate expression and without any long pauses), the student can go on to Level One Structured Stories.
- If the student has not learned enough words, use the Beach story to teach the words, using repetition and flash cards. However, do not introduce Structured Stories until the student has finished Level Two of the Language Experience stories.

Next Steps

You now have taken the student through a sample of each of the parts of the Triangle Approach:

- Phonics/phonemic awareness
- Language experience story by student
- Reading of structured stories by others

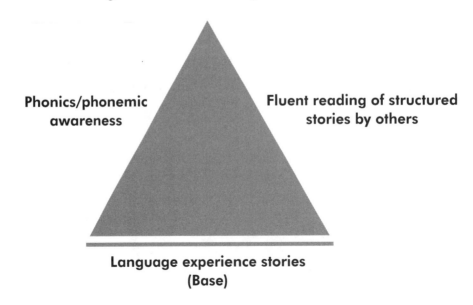

Phonics/phonemic awareness

Fluent reading of structured stories by others

Language experience stories
(Base)

Although the assessment has given you some numerical guidelines, you will gather the most helpful information on the student by closely observing her during the assessment. For example, does she make wild guesses when she doesn't know a word? When she makes mistakes on words, do the mistakes begin with the same letter as the written word? (That may indicate that she pays attention to the beginning of the words.) Notice whether she can learn the word if you model it once or twice, indicating that she can learn well from hearing a model. The teaching levels can be flexible, and you may need to adjust the student's placement in them as you continue teaching.

Triangle Reading Assessment (Informal)

Score Sheet

Alphabet Letters (Entrance to the phonemic awareness/phonics section)	List letters identified with no hesitation	List letters incorrectly identified	Evaluation Level One 90% of letters read correctly—place at Level One.* (Less than 90% letters correctly named—place at Preliminary Level) *You will probably need to pretest each objective in the phonemic awareness/phonics section to know how much emphasis is needed on that subject.
Language Experience Story	Words in student language story	Words read correctly	Evaluation Level One 75-80% words correct (3 or fewer words correctly read—place at Preliminary Level or Teacher Story)
Fluent Reading of Others' Stories	Words in others' story ("The Beach")	Words read correctly	Evaluation Level One 3 content words + 3 sight words read correctly (Less than 6 words read correctly—place at Preliminary Level)

If the student places on Level One for any of the parts of the Triangle Approach, she may be able to learn on a higher level. Start your instruction on Level One, but if it seems easy for her, try one lesson on Level Two to see if she is able to learn at that level.

In each of the Phonemic Awareness/Phonics sections, you should try three items from the Evaluation level with the student before you start the lessons for that subject. It is possible that a student may understand some of the later concepts even if she needs work on earlier subjects. For example, the student might understand how to divide words into syllables but need work on r-controlled vowels.

If you have been working with the student for some time, you may not need to give the entire Informal Assessment because you are already aware of her skills. However, you should still give the student three items from the Evaluation of each level of the Phonemic Awareness/Phonics section before you start the lessons on that section.

As you progress with reading instruction, your student(s) may experience all three parts of the Triangle Approach to reading. At first, you will just do language experience stories and phonics. When you reach Level Two in Language Experience Stories, you should start on the Structured Stories by Other Authors. It is up to you as to how you distribute the instruction. You may want to do all three parts in one day—for example, if you only meet with the student for a long period once a week. Most students do better if the instruction is done in small periods of time on a daily or three-times-a-week basis, however. A lot of the instruction depends on how long the student can stay focused and continue to respond.

It is quite possible that your student(s) will not be on the same level in each of the three parts in the Triangle Approach. For example, a student might be on Level Three in Phonemic Awareness/Phonics, on Level Two in Language Experiences, and on Level One in Structured Stories by Others. You can tailor the instruction to that student's skills more individually with this kind of a flexible approach. You should not work with more than three students during the same teaching session so you can individualize each student's instruction in all three areas.

The Triangle Approach can be adapted to group instruction by having the students do a common experience and then writing a language experience story about it in a group. However, you won't be able to see the individual growth or weaknesses of these older students as well as in a very small group.

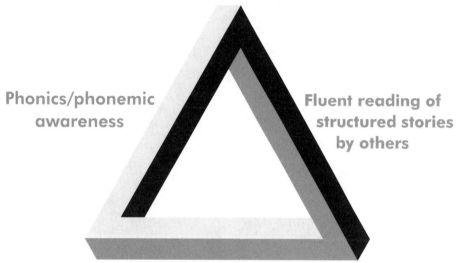

Phonics/phonemic
awareness

Fluent reading of
structured stories
by others

**Language experience stories
(Base)**

Chapter 3: General Instructions for Making Language Experience Stories
- Basic Steps
  - Choose a Story Topic
  - Plan Out and Talk through the Story
  - Put the Story in Writing
  - Illustrate the Story
- Incorporating Language Experience Stories into Reading Instruction
  - First Session
  - Before the Next Lesson
  - Next Session
  - When to Move On
- Reading Levels of Language Experience Stories
- Recording the Student's Progress
- Review of Lesson Procedures
- Story Forms and Sample Stories

Chapter 4: Characteristics and Samples of Language Experience Stories
- Level One Language Experience Stories
- Level Two Language Experience Stories
- Level Three Language Experience Stories

General Instructions for Making Language Experience Stories

I f you have done an informal assessment as described in Chapter 2, you will have a general idea of how to create a language experience story. If you have not assessed the student with the language experience part of the Triangle Reading Informal Assessment, look at the teacher story on page 9 for an overview.

Basic Steps

1. *Help the student choose a story topic:* Tell the student you are going to help him write a story about something that happened to him (or that interests him). Ask him what he would like to write about.
2. *Plan out the story:* Ask the student to tell you about his experience.
3. *Put the story in writing:* Write or type one to three sentences per page (for Level One).
4. *Illustrate the story*—preferably with the student's help.

The sections below offer more guidance on each of these steps.

Step 1: Choose a Story Topic

Ideally, the student will suggest something that he would like to write about. If he can't think of a topic and you know him well, you can suggest recent experiences or topics of interest that he might enjoy reading about. You may want to talk to his parents for suggestions about topics.

Otherwise, here are some *suggestions for topics for language experience stories:*
- A trip, party, or special event (can be illustrated with actual photos)
- Making any simple food such as pizza, punch drink, or brownies
- A favorite sport or one of the players (you can use websites about the game or players for pictures)
- Music, TV, or movie stars (you can use teen magazines, soap opera magazines, etc. for pictures)
- Going to the grocery store or the mall
- Hanging out (with pictures of friends)
- Video games (with pictures from covers or website)
- A family pet, and what the student likes to do with his pet
- Job or volunteer activities
- Friends/relatives (My Grandma, My Best Friend, My Niece)
- Prompts: My favorite holiday is…. My hobby is…. My favorite season is…. The best gift I got was….

Step 2: Plan Out and Talk through the Story

- Once your student has chosen a topic, you can begin the story-writing process by saying, "Tell me what happened" or "Tell me about …."
- If the student doesn't tell the events in sequence, help him figure out what happened first, second, etc. Or if he proposes a topic, but then gets stuck on what to say, ask questions to flesh out the details. (For example, "Why do you like Taylor Lautner? What movies is he in?")
- If the student is not very verbal, or only uses 1 - 2 word utterances, write exactly what he says at first. For example: "My dog. Black. Lick me. Funny." Later you may try to expand the student's utterances. It is possible that he can understand longer phrases than he expresses. Some students are able to verbally expand their language by seeing it written. If the student will only read the words he has dictated, ask him to point to the word(s) you have added. Do not correct his grammar unless it is absolutely not understandable. You need to have his permission to change the phrase or sentence. If his sentences are too long or unclear, guide the student to use short sentences. For example, say, "Oh, do you mean . . . ?" (a short version of his words).
- For more complex or longer stories, you may want to use the Story Forms on pages 25-30 or in Appendix A1 (in the back of the book or on CD) to record the student's ideas and keep your own record of the story without pictures. The three types of forms are for experience stories, sequence stories, and descriptive stories.
- I have found that stories are more interesting to students if they contain a little humor. For example, the story about building a huge sandwich is more fun if you laugh about the sandwich being so big that the narrator can't get it in his mouth. When stories include humor, you may be able to tell whether the student understands the content of the story or can predict what the funny ending will be. Students also seem to respond more to a surprise ending.

Look at the sample language stories included at each level of the Language Experience Stories section in Chapter 4. They show a development from simple, short stories to longer and more complex stories.

Step 3: Put the Story in Writing

- The day that you first write the story with the student (steps 1 and 2), you will want to produce a rough draft of the story so you can read it with him at least two times on the spot.
- How do you write down a language experience story?
    - First, you can simply handwrite each sentence of the story toward the bottom of a sheet of paper. Print clearly and leave extra space between words so that it is clear where each word stops and ends. If you have time, you may illustrate the story with stick figure-type drawings. You can have the student illustrate his story with his own drawings before the next lesson session or you can cut out the drawings and paste them on the original story. Leave plenty of space on the pages for pictures.
    - Second, you can type the story on the computer, scrolling down so each sentence is toward the bottom of the page. Beginning stories are often done in Microsoft Power Point because the format lends itself to becoming a book. Most of the learning experience books I have seen are created in Ariel or Comic Sans font. You may have to experiment with the print size. Beginning books for children are published in large print because of their developing eyesight. Depending on your student's age, he may be able to read smaller print. However, I have found that double spacing the lines and leaving plenty of white space helps most struggling students. Before the next session, you can illustrate the story, as described below.

Step 4: Illustrate the Story

You actually do not have to have pictures to accompany a language experience story. Many students remember their own words without illustrations. However, many others students use the illustrations to help remember the words. One mother told me that her daughter could read unillustrated versions of her stories, but she would go to the illustrated stories and read them again and again by herself. That is an important teaching tool for students who reread their stories independently. Some students may want to read your other students' stories (as stories by other authors) when they are illustrated.

Clip Art

To illustrate language experience stories, I often use clip art pictures from Microsoft Word 7. If you have Microsoft Word on your computer, you can illustrate stories for your students' own use with the clip art that comes with the program. To use this program, first click on Insert Clip Art (Or Insert, Picture, Clip Art, if you have an older version).This brings up a side program that lets you search for the type of picture you want. You can then choose among the pictures available and insert one in the text as an illustration.

If you have access to the Boardmaker computer program, you can get black and white line drawings of almost any word. Likewise, if you have PECS symbols, they can also be used to illustrate stories.

In addition, you can often find clip art online by doing a search for "free clip art" plus the type of picture you are looking for (for example, "free clip art dog").

Drawings

An ideal way to help a student remember the words in the story is to have him draw pictures to illustrate it. See the samples of a student's drawings in the story entitled "Daniel" in Chapter 10. You can either have your student draw right on the story pages after the lesson or have him make his drawings on a separate piece of paper, then cut them out and glue them to the book pages.

If the student is not interested in illustrating the story, you can contribute drawings. You don't have to be an artist to illustrate a language experience story. You could draw stick figures and label them with spoken words. If you tell the student with humor, "This is a real picture of a horse. See—it has ears and a tail," he will be able to use the stick figure picture to help read the words. You can also draw outlines of items and figures and have the student color them.

Photos

Students are exceptionally interested when you put real pictures of them in their language experience books. You can take photos at every step of an event or experience if you know you will want to write a book about the event. Or you can use existing snapshots to come up with a storyline after the fact. You also can get all sorts of pictures from the Internet. Sources include:

- Bing Images (www.bing.com; click on "Images" at the top of the page)
- FreeFoto.com (www.freefoto.com)
- Free Stock Photos (www.freestockphotos.com)
- Google Images (www.google.com; click on "Images" at the top of the page)
- Library of Congress Prints and Photographs Reading Room (www.loc.gov/rr/print)

There are several ways to incorporate photos into a language experience story. First, if you have digital files of the photos on your picture, you can copy and paste them into the pages of your story. You may need to experiment to get the right size for the page. Most photo software has an "edit" function that lets you resize your images. Make sure you save your resized photos as a copy so you don't permanently reduce the size of a favorite photo.

You can also use photo prints in your stories. The simplest way is to first print out the story with the text at the bottom of the page, then glue or tape the photos to the page. You can also scan photos into your computer and then insert them in the story. In addition, you can use photo albums to create books. To use this method, you print out or write the text on a sheet of paper and then cut it so that the text for each page is on its own strip. Then insert the text strips with the corresponding photos into the album.

Finally, if you have the money and you want to make a really professional looking book, you can use the "photo book" option available from photo processing companies such as Snapfish and Shutterfly.

Otherwise, staple the pages together like a book and make a colorful cover. Look at the sample stories for each level of the language experience stories in Chapter 4. You can learn a lot from these actual stories.

Incorporating Language Experience Stories into Reading Instruction

Each week you work with a student on reading, you need to do two or three types of activities in the Triangle Approach:
1. Language Experience Stories
2. Phonics/Phonemic Awareness
3. Structured Stories (after the student is beyond Level One or Two in Language Experience Stories)

You are going to have the student read one language experience story many times before he has learned all the words (out of context) in the story and can read it fluently, without many pauses, with appropriate expression and understanding the content.

First Session

Each time you write a new story with the student, you should follow this general procedure.

- Follow steps 1-4, as described on pages 17-20, to write the story.
- Read the story to the student when you have finished, pointing to each word.
- Then you and the student read the story together. You read the story correctly, but do not correct the student if he makes mistakes.
- See if the student can read the story independently. Assist him with any words he is not sure of, and praise any attempts to read.
- That is probably all you can finish in one session.

Before the Next Lesson

- Before the next session, type or write the new words or words not-yet-learned on the vocabulary boxes form (called "footballs" in the Triangle Approach). (See page 31, Appendix A2, or CD for a blank form.) Cut the "footballs" apart so you have a ball for each new word. You will use these words to see if the student can identify the words outside of the context of the story.
- Illustrate the story (if possible).
- Write the vocabulary words on your copy of the language experience story.

The vocabulary words will be divided into two categories—sight words and content words:

Sight Words: A sight word is a word that a reader knows automatically without decoding the word's spelling. These words, such as those on the Dolch and the Fry word lists, make up 50-75 percent of the words in the reading material used by students. (See Appendix A3 for Fry's First 100 Sight Words.) Examples include *and, it,* and *is.* Some of these sight words have spellings that cannot be decoded by regular phonic rules. For example, *said, does,* and *laugh.* Many of these words are difficult to picture graphically. In order for students to read fluently, they must be able to read these short words automatically. It usually takes repeated uses of sight words for them to be read automatically.

Content Words: A content word may be specific to the particular story—for example, *apple, river,* and *pull.* It can frequently be pictured graphically. Content words usually give most of the meaning to the sentence.

- **Sight Words**
  out
  around
  to

- **Content Words**
  lazy
  river
  swim

Next Session

- At the next session, you read the language experience story with the student.
- Next, see how much of the story the student can read by himself.
- Repeat the story with any assistance the student needs, such as reading with him or having another student read every other sentence, etc.
- Then, throw the vocabulary footballs on the floor or table in front of the student.
- Ask the student if he can read any of the footballs in front of him and hand them to you.

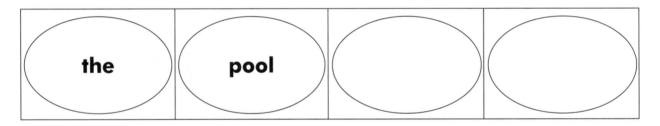

- Make two piles of words—incorrect (or omitted) and correct.
- Pick up the incorrect words and you and the student match each one to the same word in the language experience story.
- Review each word.
- Spread out the missed words in front of the student and see if he can read any of them independently now.

You need to read the story and play the football game repeatedly until the student really knows the words, both in the story and in isolation. The student needs to know that repeated oral readings of the story are important to learning to read, even if it is a little boring. The student should be able to orally read the story fluently after repeated readings. Comprehension should not be a problem, since the story was written by the student about his own activity. However, you can ask some questions if you are not sure the student knows the content. You will work more on reading comprehension in the structured stories by other authors.

When to Move On

In general, when the student can read the story fluently and can read over 90 percent of the words in isolation, it is time to make another story. However, if an important event happens before you have finished the first story, write the new story and continue to read both the first story *and* the second story. Occasionally reread old stories with the student to show him how much he has progressed and to review the vocabulary.

Reading Levels of Language Experience Stories

You do not have to know the exact grade level of the stories you write. If you look closely at the sample stories at each level, you will probably do well. If the student does not learn the words after several sessions, you have probably made the story too difficult. Sometimes a student can read a higher level story if he knows a lot about the subject or has an intense interest in it.

If you need to know the reading level, there are several readability scores that can be used to calculate grade levels of written text. They are mainly based on the length of words and sentences used, as well as the average number of syllables per word. They often give a score equivalent to a grade level.

You can figure out a Flesch-Kincaid readability score on the language experience stories you write by entering the text in Microsoft Word. Do the spelling and grammar check. A box will pop up giving the statistics for a Flesch-Kincaid readability score. A 0 score indicates a level before first grade. First and second grade are indicated by scores of 1 or 2. A numerical readability score from 1 to 100 is also given, with higher numbers representing better readability.

The Flesch-Kincaid score does not show other features that determine whether the reading material is appropriate for a beginning reader. These features include the use of: simple phonics principles, pictures that tell part of the story, repetition of words and phrases, predictable content, and regularity of spelling. Use the Flesch-Kincaid score only as a broad guide to the level of the stories you have been writing for the student.

If you are seeking out published stories for your students and reading levels are important to you, you should know that other authors have developed more comprehensive reading levels that are not as easily quantifiable as readability scores. For example, whole language developers Fountas and Pinnell have 13+ levels corresponding to kindergarten to second grade reading level. Rigby Publishers have 22 levels for the same grade levels. Reading Recovery's intensive early program has 22 levels. These levels are based on all the areas described above.

You do not have to figure out reading levels for each of the student's language experience stories. Information on determining reading level is only given here in the event you have questions about the sequencing of the student's language stories.

Recording the Student's Progress

You will need to record the vocabulary words as the student learns them. After the student has read a new word three times in isolation (not just in the story), you can cross out that word on the record of sight and the content words that are listed on the language experience form:

Sight Words		Content Words	
my is		grandpa years	
with us		live(s) loud	

Another way to keep a record is to save the word squares (footballs) that your student(s) has learned. If you are doing curriculum-based measurement, you might want to test new words every few weeks to show progress. You can cross out the words on your copy of the vocabulary form or check them off on the actual footballs. At intervals, you should check the list of Fry words in Appendix A3 to see if the student is learning appropriate sight words.

Review of Lesson Procedures

- Discuss events or interests with the student and choose one event or interest for a language experience story.
- Write the story as the student talks. You can type the story with a computer or print the story clearly in handwriting on paper or on a chart, if you are working with several students. Use one of the story planning forms (at the end of this chapter) if the story is more complex.
- Read the story with the student.
- Let the student try to read it independently.
- Explain any missed words to the student.
- Before the next lesson, make a new book with the student's words and add pictures to the book. Write the new words on the vocabulary word form (footballs) in Appendix A2.
- Cut apart the word footballs and put them on the floor or the table in front of the student.
- Have the student read the words he knows in isolation. Put the incorrect and correct words into separate piles.
- Locate the missed words in the story and compare the "football" word to its use in the story.
- Keep having the student repeat the language experience story until he can read it with accuracy or with only one word missed. Even after you and your student have written another language experience story, you should have the student read the first story occasionally.
- Have the student read the story to parents or friends.
- Have the student start reading Structured Stories by Other Authors (Chapter 10).

Experience Story Form

Title:

Author:

Describe the setting:

Activities:

Problem:

Outcome:

Sight Words	Content Words

Experience Story Form

Sample Story (at Level Two)

Title: Swim

Author: Steve

Describe the setting: I went to the Swim Center. The Swim Center has 3 pools.
One pool is round. It is called the Lazy River.
The water in the pool goes around and around.

Activities: I swim and swim and swim on the Lazy River.
It was time to go home.

Problem: I could not get out of the pool.
The water moved me around and around—fast.

Outcome: "Help," I yelled. My friend pulled me out of the water.
That Lazy River was <u>not</u> lazy with me!

Sight Words			Content Words		
of	the	has	Swim	Center	round
with	no	could	lazy	river	around
out	to	me	time	pull(ed)	one
that	on	was	pool	goes	fast
went	my	has	home	friend	three
in	it		water	call(ed)	like
			help	move(d)	yell(ed)

Sequence Story Form *(Making Something—recipes, objects, etc.)*

Title:

Author:

Setting:

Sequence:

Outcome:

Sight Words	Content Words

Sequence Story Form *(Making Something—recipes, objects, etc.)*

Sample Story (at Level Two)

Title: Brownies

Author: Allison

Setting: I want brownies.
I need water, brownie mix, oil, a bowl, measuring spoons.

Sequence: I open the mix.
I put it in a bowl.
I put oil (3 tablespoons) in the bowl
I put water (2 tablespoons) in the bowl.
I stir and stir all the stuff.
I pour the stuff in a baking pan.
Oh, I forgot to get out a baking pan!
I put the baking pan in the oven.

Outcome: I get the pan out of the oven.
I eat brownies.

Sight Words			Content Words		
I	a	it	brownie(s)	bowl	spoon(s)
out	and	need	stir	oil	water
put	in	oh	mix	measure(ing)	open
get			forgot	stuff	eat
			oven	tablespoon	pan
			pour		

Note: The teacher added the measurements in case some other student uses the story as a guide to actually making brownies.

Description Story Form *(person, animal, etc.)*

Title:

Author:

Identification:

Description:

Sum up:

Sight Words	Content Words

Description Story Form *(person, animal, etc.)*

Sample Story (at Level One)

Title: Grandpa

Author: Laurie

Identification: My grandpa is 60 years old. He lives with us.

Description: My grandpa is tall. He is bald on top.
He has a loud voice.
He yells at me, but not mad.
I like to play Frisbee with him.
Sometimes he don't catch the Frisbee.
That makes me laugh.

Sum up: I like my grandpa.
He likes me too.

Sight Words			Content Words		
is	he	him	grandpa	play	laugh
at	not	my	live(s)	bald	years old
on	sometimes	me	Frisbee	catch	tall
with	has	like	voice	loud	top
don't	us	a	mad	yells	
to	too				

Vocabulary Words Form (Footballs)

Story:

Author:

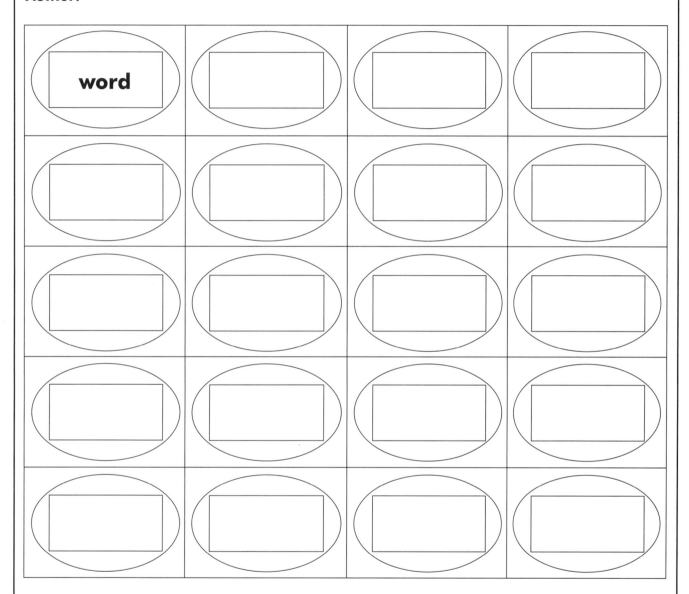

Type or print new or not-yet-learned words in the boxes and cut them out. Put words in a small, clear plastic bag and label with the name of the story. Throw the word squares onto a table or the floor, calling them footballs. Ask the student to pick up the words he or she knows and say them to you. Make two piles of words—correct and not correct. Review the incorrect words with the student. Show the student where the word is in the story. See if the student can read the words independently after the review.

Note: If you make two copies of the football sheet, you can use the copy to keep track of the vocabulary the student is learning instead of recording the words on the experience story form.

Characteristics and Samples of Language Experience Stories

Language experience stories should be in the student's language and taken from his or her experiences. Of course, you cannot control the words of the story that the student dictates. However, the parent or teacher can help make the stories more readable by sequencing them from very easy to more difficult using some of the characteristics used by reading series. For example, the characteristics of Level One stories in this book are similar to those of the beginning whole language stories. They are interesting to young beginning readers. We want to take advantages of their good teaching value, but adapt them to the interests of older students.

As you develop stories on a given level for a particular student, you don't need to use all the characteristics that are listed for that student's level. Just keep them in mind as you are encouraging the student to expand her stories.

Forms to help you plan language experience stories at all levels are available in the Appendix. They are also included on the CD in the back of the book.

Tip: Students often tell run-on stories with many sentences connected by the word *and*. You can shorten the run-on sentences as you write what the student says by saying, "That is really a new sentence. Can we write down…[the student's words as a second sentence]?

Level One Language Experience Stories

Characteristics of Level One Beginning Reading Text

1. Short sentences (2-7 words)
2. Mostly one-syllable words (with a few two-syllable words)
3. Frequent repetition of new words

4. Predictability of the story
5. Topics and content of stories age appropriate for secondary level students
6. Sight words included are mostly from pre-primer developmental levels (See Appendix A3 for a list of Fry's First 100 Sight Words)
7. Pictures tell part of the story
8. Blank lines are left between each line of text
9. When possible, story has an interesting, imaginative end

These are the characteristics that Level One Stories would *ideally* include. Obviously, when a student is telling you a story about her experiences or interests, she will not be aware of these characteristics. You do not want to alter her original story very much, but you can guide her to use shorter words and sentences and also add pictures and blank lines. Note that Part 3 of this book (Structured Stories) contains stories designed in Level One style using the above characteristics with the addition of vocabulary that builds on previous stories.

Examples of Level One Stories

The following story examples are actual language experience stories written by older beginning readers I have worked with. They have been modified for privacy reasons. My intent in including them is not to provide you with ready-made stories to read with your students. Rather, I am including these stories to give you an idea of how age-appropriate content can be combined with simpler language. They also give me an opportunity to discuss issues related to word choice, grammar, and other issues that sometimes crop up when writing language experience stories.

Discussion of Story in Example 1:

- The story is not really pleasant, but it is real. You should not censor your student's stories just because they are on topics you don't particularly care for. The point is for the student to write about something that interests him or her.
- Pictures carry most of the story. If the student had photos of himself hunting with his father, they would have made better illustrations, but the clip art pictures do convey the situation.
- The story is under first grade level, according to the Flesch-Kincaid scale.
- Words and phrases are repeated: hunting, deer, I get my … wet. I guided the student to repeat words by the questions I asked.
- The last sentence is ungrammatical. I did not correct it because that is the way the student said it, and it was his story.

Note: This story, like all examples in this section, has been condensed to one page. The original story may have had only one or two sentences per page.

It may also have been just one page long, including illustrations, if the student could read it that way. Some teachers like to make one copy of the story for the student and one for themselves to keep as a record. I find it very convenient to include the sight and content words on my copy of the story in small print so I can keep track of the vocabulary and check off words as the student learns them.

If you have several students, you will probably want to make an alphabetized master list of the words used and learned by each student. A parent with one student can probably remember the content and sight words her child has learned.

Level One, Example 1: Experience Story

Hunting

My Dad and I go hunting.

We go hunting for deer.

It rains hard.

I get my face wet.

I get my feet wet.

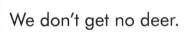

We don't get no deer.

Sight Words			Content Words		
we	no	don't	feet	wet	face
get	my	I	rains	hard	Dad
if	go	for	hunt(ing)	deer	

Sample Vocabulary Word Form

Football Game for "Hunting" Story

my	Dad	and	I
go	hunting	we	for
it	rains	get	hard
face	feet	wet	don't
no	deer		

Discussion of Word Form in Example 1:

- There are many easy sight words such as *it, no, I* because the student was a beginner at language experience stories. Once the student has learned these sight words, you don't have to include them on the footballs unless you want him to review them. Sometimes, however, it is good to include some easy words on the footballs to make sure the student is partially successful in reading them.
- Only capitalize words on footballs if they are proper nouns. Do not capitalize the word just because it is capitalized as the first word in a sentence in the story.

Level One, Example 2: Sequence Story

Pancakes

I get the mix.

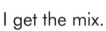

I get the milk.

I stir.

I cook the pancakes.

I eat the pancakes.

Sight Words			Content Words		
I	get	them	mix	milk	pancake(s)
the			stir	cook	eat

Discussion of Sequence Story in Example 2:

■ This story illustrates how the steps in preparing food or making something can be used to make a simple sequence story.

■ It is easy to include repetition in these types of stories. This story repeats sentences, just changing one word. "I get the _____." ; "I _____ the pancakes." You can easily prompt the student to repeat words when initially writing the question by asking her questions.

■ Again, the reading level is under first grade, according to the Flesh-Kincaid scale.

■ You can point out picture or real cues (such as the milk carton) to help the student remember the story.

Discussion of (Short) Story in Example 3:

■ You would probably want to have the student talk more about this situation. However, as short as the story is, it is still a valid language experience story. You may want to include one picture per sentence to make a small book.

■ In stories such as this that are about a particular individual, it is helpful to use pictures of the person, especially if the student is literal and will say, "That's not Arnie." For most students, it is okay to mix photos with clip art when illustrating as long as you explain the mix to them.

■ Note that that there was a change in tense from the beginning of the story ("They wanted Uncle Arnie") to the ending ("Arnie is not here"). You should not change the student's grammar unless you are on Level Three and improving grammar is a goal for that student.

■ The story uses the word *cops* instead of *policemen* because that is the language the student uses. If the story is going home to parents, I might put the more acceptable word after the student word in parenthesis. Although I accept the student's slang, I do not accept swear words when writing a language experience story with a student.

Discussion of Description Story Example 4:

■ This is an example of a story written about something that the student has an intense interest in. The teacher probably does not know the meaning of all the words in the story. The teacher could ask the student to explain *ollies* and *kick flips* when writing the story. Later the teacher may want to add the student's description of those words to the story.

■ There are not as many pictures in this story because they wouldn't add much to the content of the story.

Level One, Example 3: Experience Story

Trouble

The cops came to my house.

They wanted Uncle Arnie.

Arnie is not here.

Arnie must be in trouble.

Sight Words			Content Words		
the	came	to	cops	house	Uncle Arnie
my	they	want	trouble		
is	came	to			
my	not	there			
in					

Level One, Example 4: Description Story

Title: My Skateboard

Author: Hugo

Identification: My skateboard is my favorite thing.

Description: The deck is the top of my skateboard.

I can do tricks on my skateboard.

I can do kick flips.

I can do ollies.

I can make my skateboard lift over bumps.

Sum up: My skateboard is the best there is.

Sight Words			Content Words		
I	the	my	skateboard	kick flips	ollies
do	make	over	lift	bump	sidewalk
there	is	best	top	trick(s)	favorite
on	lots	can	thing	deck	

Level Two Language Experience Stories

Students may be ready for Level Two stories when they tell stories that include sentences with four or more words. They will probably also write longer stories and use more words with several syllables in their stories.

Characteristics of Level Two Beginning Reading Text

1. Sentences that are 4 to 9 words long
2. Three to 8 lines of text per page
3. Sentences may have clauses. The order of the sentence will vary from regular subject, verb, object form. For example: *Before the game*, the cheerleaders met in their locker room.
4. Continued repetition and predictability
5. Variety of types of stories, such as science stories or fantasies
6. Topics and content of stories age-appropriate for secondary level students
7. Pictures carry less of the content
8. Sight words according to primer developmental levels

Again, the language experience stories you write with your students won't necessarily contain all of these characteristics, since the content and complexity will depend on the student's activities and interests, as well as the sophistication of her speech. In Part 3 of this book, you will find structured stories at Level Two that do contain all these characteristics, with the addition of vocabulary that builds on previous stories.

Sometimes a student does not speak in 4- to 9-word sentences or omits little words such as *the* or *to*. Susan Buckley, a psychologist in the United Kingdom, has documented that students with Down syndrome can improve their length of utterances by reading the words they usually omit in written material. If you have a student who omits words, you might try writing the stories as she dictates them, and then before the next lesson, add one or two usually omitted words to the finished story. See if the student can read those additional words. If she does not, say the word and ask her to touch it on the story page.

Examples of Level Two Stories

Discussion of Experience Story Level Two, Example 1:

- Some of the sentences are longer than in a Level One story (5-9 words). If the student did not initially make sentences that were this long, you could prompt her to add details. (What kind of hat? What kind of water?) Do not question the student if it will interrupt the flow of her story.
- There are several events in the story (family members getting relief from the heat, mowing the lawn, Dad spraying with the hose, revenge by the student).
- Pictures do not illustrate every sentence.
- Repetition of words is still used.
- Note that the type can probably be smaller than in Level One stories, but it is still important to leave white space so the story appears more friendly.
- This story is written at the first-grade level.

Level Two, Example 1: Experience Story

Hot

It is July and it is very hot outside.

The sun is bright and there are no clouds in the sky.

My family is outdoors in the yard this morning.

My Dad, my Mom, and my sister are hot.

I am really, really hot!

My Dad gets a big fan for the garage.
He is going to fix the car.

The fan keeps him cool.

Mom gets a hat to keep the sun off her face. She feels cooler.

My sister gets to go down in the basement. It is cool there.

I get nothing!
I get to mow the lawn.

It is a long, hot job, but I finally finish.

My Dad gets the water hose.

He sprays me with cold water.

I'm going to get him back.

I fill a whole bucket with water.

Then I get Dad wet—really wet!.

I am not hot anymore!

Level Two, Example 2: Fantasy Story

Title: My Alien Friend

Author: Jamal

Describe the setting: I was in a food court when an alien fell from thin air.
He crashed through the ceiling.

Activities: The alien landed on my lunch.
He said, "Sorry, I will buy you a lunch."
He was green and ten feet tall.
His skin was wrinkly. He was nice inside, even though he looked scary.
I said, "My name is Jamal."
He said, "My name is 72394."

Problem: What can a alien and me do for fun?
He doesn't bowl, or ride a bike, or play Spud.

Outcome: We went to a movie named Mission to Mars.
After the movie, 72394 got homesick. So he went home.

Sight Words			**Content Words**		
we	said	went	Mars	green	food court
what	doesn't	do	feet	movie	mission
for	or	is	name(d)	bowl	Mars
he	was	through	fun	alien	bike
so	sorry	will	play	ten	tall
you	at	me	ride	Spud	fun
a	got	can	skin	inside	wrinkly
			thin	scary	nice
			crash(ed)	fell	ceiling
			homesick	lunch	buy

Discussion of Fantasy Level Two Language Story:

- A language experience story doesn't have to be a true experience. Students often have vivid imaginations, which they can use when writing Level Two and Level Three stories.
- Notice the variety of content words that were needed in this fantasy story. The student should already have many of the sight words as part of her vocabulary.
- A Level Two story may have fewer pictures to illustrate it, as in this story, or the student may want to draw many pictures for her story. (See student story, "Daniel," in Chapter 10.)
- This story has a beginning, a middle with several events, and an ending. It is written at the 1.9 grade level, according to the Flesch-Kincaid scale.

Level Three Language Experience Stories

Characteristics of Level Three Beginning Reading Text

1. Longer stories with a beginning, middle events, and an end
2. Longer sentences of 8 to 12 words
3. More multisyllabic words
4. Topics and content of stories age-appropriate for secondary level students and above
5. Stories may have a plot and chapters
6. More irregular, difficult words are used
7. Pictures less frequent and more general

In Level Three, the teacher still writes down the student's own stories. However, you can combine some of the short sentences to make longer and more complex sentences. (Of course, you need to get the student's permission to do that.) By this time, your student should be dictating stories with a clear beginning, middle events, and an end. If not, you may have to prompt her with questions like "What happened after that?" It is easier to write Level Three stories if you have a theme and have done some planning ahead of time. Say you are going to take a group of students on a trip to the corn maze. You can plan several parts of the trip and take pictures at important times. Other things that are important to the students may also happen and the students will tell you about them later.

It is best if the student can tell her story all in one day. If it takes more than a day to write a long Level Three story, you should divide it into several chapters and write it over the course of two days.

Part Three of this book offers structured stories designed in Level Three style using the above characteristics with the addition of vocabulary that builds on previous stories.

Level Three Example: Experience Story

Out of Work

My Dad lost his job. He used to help build office buildings.
People are not building office buildings in our city—right now.

Dad's face looked sad when he told us about losing his job. Dad said, "Eileen's father and Mr. Dean from down the street also lost their jobs."

Mom went up and hugged Dad. My sister Sue started crying.
"What will we do? How will we eat?"

Dad smiled and said, "Sue, we have food to eat. We need to get together as a family and talk about what to do."

We sat down at the kitchen table and talked.
I don't remember what we talked about.
    I just kept on thinking, "My Dad lost his job! My Dad lost his job!

      I won't be able to go to the water park with my class.
        It costs a lot of money."

My Dad tried to find another job.
    He read the newspaper and called people.
        He said, "No one is hiring new workers.
           I'm glad that I have unemployment money
           coming from the job—even if it is not very much."

Mom was working part time at the grocery store.
    She asked her boss if she could work more hours.
        Now she has to work later in the day.

She talked to me about me babysitting with my sister Sue
    for two hours after school.
        I said okay.

Mom talked to my sister Sue about obeying me when I babysat.
That is important!

I am cutting the grass for Mrs. Beacham.
    I may have enough money to go to the water park.

My Dad is still looking for a job, but he is working part time delivering pizzas.

Sometimes he brings home a pizza for us.
We are doing okay because we are working as a family.

Sight Words			Content Words		
right	kept on	now	job	lost	office
our	how	when	eat	people	need
able	will	just	told	family	sad
also	about		think(ing)	hug(ged)	water park
			cry(ing)	money	now
			class	smile(d)	remember
			together	costs	use(d)
			table	building	sat
			city	kitchen	said
			talk	food	start(ed)

Already learned: my, as, it, with, at, we, get, do, up, their, our, not, to, are, what, now, went

Discussion of Level Three Experience Story Example:

At this level of story writing, you may ask the student some questions to expand the story. However, it is still the student's story and you should generally not correct the student's grammar unless the story is not understandable.

You may be able to use smaller print now; however, white spacing is still needed. I often arrange the sentences as if they were a poem. You can vary the sentence indentation to give added interest to the story.

If this particular story were completed at school, parents might think the topic was an invasion of privacy. If working on a story on a sensitive topic like this, a teacher should probably call the parent and talk to them about it. However, the situation is certainly something that is important to the student, so it should not be ignored,

Notice that there are now many more content words to be learned than sight words because there is more content to be learned. The student is getting to the stage of transitioning from learning to read to reading to learn.

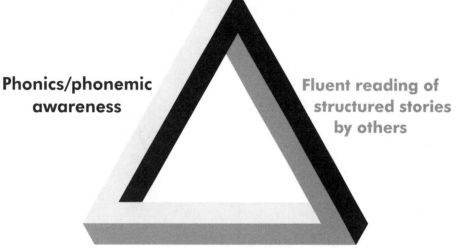

Phonics/phonemic
awareness

Fluent reading of
structured stories
by others

Language experience stories
(Base)

Chapter 5: Introduction to Phonemic Awareness/Phonics
- Are Phonemic Awareness and Phonics the Same?
- Scope and Sequence of Typical Phonics Programs
- Preliminary Level Phonemic Awareness
- Letter Names
- Rhymes

Chapter 6: Level One Phonics
- Letter Sounds—Consonants
- Short Vowels—/a/
- Short Vowels—/i/
- Short Vowels—/o/ and /u/
- Short Vowels—/e/

Chapter 7: Level Two Phonics
- Long Vowels—Silent E
- Long Vowels—Two Vowels Together
- C and G
- Blend Sounds
- Word Endings—Plurals, /ed/, and /ing/

Chapter 8: Level Three Phonics
- R-Controlled Vowels
- Multisyllabic Words—Syllables
- Multisyllabic Words—Prefixes, Suffixes, and Contractions

Chapter 9: Optional Level Four Phonics
- Syllable Division Rules

Introduction to Phonemic Awareness/Phonics

Are Phonemic Awareness and Phonics the Same?

Strictly speaking, *phonemic awareness (PA)* consists of recognizing oral sounds (not written symbols) and being able to manipulate them. For example, a child who has phonemic awareness might hear the word *go* and be able to tell you that it has the "guh" sound at the beginning of the word. He could recognize the sounds of the endings of words and recognize and make rhymes. He may also be able to add or delete sounds from a word.

In contrast, *phonics* consists of relating letters to the sounds. That is, it includes the ability to look at letters in a written word and "sound out" that word, as well as to translate spoken words into letters. Someone who has an understanding of phonics not only understands the sounds that each letter in an alphabet can make, but also understands rules related to how different arrangements of vowels and consonants affect the letter sounds (e.g., *dot* vs. *dote*), the irregularities of decoding, and syllabification.

In April 2000, the National Reading Panel released a report summarizing research findings on learning to read. The panel determined that effective instruction includes teaching children to hear and manipulate the sounds in words (phonemic awareness), and teaching that these sounds are represented by letters that can be used to translate printed text (phonics) (Shanahan, 2006). However, research demonstrates that phonemic awareness taught *with* letters is more effective than phonemic awareness taught *without* letters (International Reading Association, 2002). Thus, phonemic awareness and phonics are often taught together, especially for older learners (McShane, 2005).

Scope and Sequence of Typical Phonics Programs

The commercially available phonics programs used in schools usually teach phonics in a systematic way. Some reading programs such as the Wilson Reading System (1988, 2007), Orton-Gillingham-based Reading Programs such as the Slingerland Institute for Literacy (1977, 1998), and the Stevenson Learning Skills (2002) categorize vowel (V) and consonant (C) patterns by syllable types:

- Closed Syllable (word ends in consonant) - CVC: e.g., *bat*
  - ➤ one vowel per syllable
  - ➤ vowel usually short
- Open Syllable (ends in vowel) - CV, CCV; e.g., *me, flu*
  - ➤ one vowel per syllable
  - ➤ vowel usually long
  - ➤ few words in this pattern
- Vowel Consonant (with silent e) - VCe; e.g., *cake*
  - ➤ first vowel usually long
  - ➤ /e/ is silent
- Double Vowel (in closed syllable) - CVVC; e.g., *leaf*
  - ➤ first vowel is usually long
  - ➤ second vowel is usually silent
- Consonant LE—CLE; e.g., *table*
  - ➤ e is silent
  - ➤ consonant is blended with L (also explained as reversing the *le* to *el*)
- R-Controlled vowel—VR; e.g., *bird, car*
  - ➤ vowel is neither long nor short
  - ➤ /ar/, /or/, /er/, /ir/, and /ur/ can all sound like /er/ in *her*

It is good for parents or teachers to know the syllable types in order to sequence the student's learning, but it is not necessary for the student to be able to recite the syllable types to be able to read fluently.

The Triangle Approach to reading covers all the syllable types above, in basically the same order, but without identifying the syllable types directly. See the phonemic awareness/phonics table of contents to see the scope and sequence for the Triangle Approach to reading used in this book.

Preliminary Level Phonemic Awareness

If you did the informal assessment in Chapter 2, you tested your student on letter knowledge. If he was not able to identify at least 90 percent of the letters, you should begin your phonemic awareness/phonics lessons with letter names. (Remember, however, that you should still be doing Language Experience stories with him, even if he scored on the preliminary level of phonemic awareness/phonics.)

Students who are just starting out on Level One may be able to read some sight words—words such as *McDonalds, Cheerios, stop,* and their names. They may not, however, be able to substitute a sound at the beginning or end of words they already know.

They may not be able to separate out the various sounds that make a word. You want them to be able to hear the beginning and ending sounds in words and to be able to tell whether words rhyme.

In research findings, letter knowledge had a high correlation with beginning reading success. It is not necessary for the student to be able to identify all the letter names before you work on letter sounds, but the letter names will make it easier to proceed with reading instruction. A lesson for teaching letter naming follows.

Lesson One: Letter Names

Learning letter names is principally a memorization task. The student may need to practice the names many times or have a visual or auditory cue to help him remember. Tasks that use more than one sense such as tactile and visual cues may help the memory for letter names.

The consonants normally have only one sound and should be taught first. It may help to have a picture of a common item that begins with the letter.

Objective: The student will correctly name the letters of the alphabet.

Materials:

- Cardstock paper or regular computer paper (if only one student)
- Letter Name Flashcards from Appendix B1 (or CD)
- Results from the letter naming test in the Triangle Reading Assessment

Success Step: Have the student name or point to letters that you know he knows (from the Reading Assessment).

Procedure:

- Run off the pictures on cardstock or regular paper.
- Cut out the pictures and the letter and name of the picture.

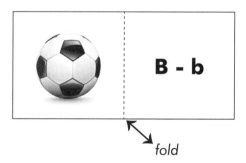

fold

- Make flashcards by folding over letter pictures from the Appendix or CD so the picture is on one side and the letter is on the other side. You can also paste the pictures on half of a 3x5 card and write the letter on the back of the card.

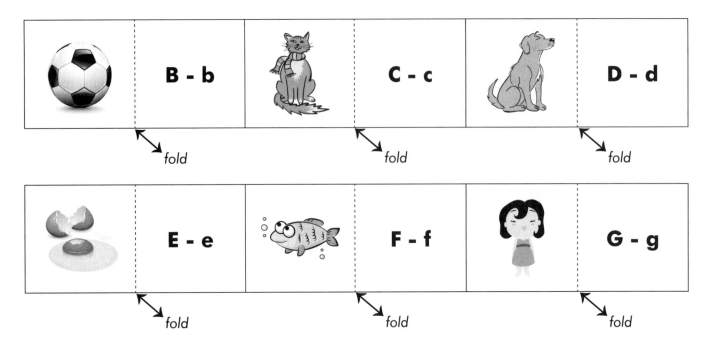

- Using the flashcards of the letters the student identified incorrectly in the assessment, show the student two consonant cards, name them, and have him say the key word from each picture.
- Repeat the procedure with two more consonant cards until most of the letters are learned. (This may occur over the course of many sessions.)
- Have the student practice with the flashcards.
- If the student needs to learn alphabetical order, teach the alphabet song to the tune of "Twinkle, Twinkle Little Star."

 ## Activities/Games

Flashcard ABC Game
- Paste the pictures on half-sized index cards or photocopy them on cardstock and cut into flashcards.
- Write the appropriate upper- and lower-case letter on the back of each card.
- Stack the cards in a pile with only the letters showing.
- One student (or the teacher) names the letter on the first card. Then he turns the card over and checks his answer by looking at the picture. The teacher may need to monitor the answers.
- If the student names the letter correctly, he receives the card.
- The student with the most cards wins.
- The teacher uses the incorrectly named cards for re-teaching.

Generalization Activities
- Give each student a page of the newspaper. Have the student highlight the letters the teacher names on the newspaper.
- Write appropriate abbreviations for common organizations such as NFL, CNN, CBS, and NBC and have the student name the letters.
- Have the student name letters on road signs, ads, or packages.

Starfall Activity

Use the computer program Starfall to work on the letter names that the student needs to know.

- Load the Starfall program from the Internet: www.starfall.com.
- Bring up the #1 Starfall program - "ABCs: Let's Get Ready to Read." Click to bring up the screen with all the letters.
- Click on the letter you want the student to learn.
- The program shows the capital letter and the lower case letter, names them, and sometimes shows a picture. Have the student repeat the name of the letter several times.
- When the student clicks the arrow below the picture, the program gives the letter sound (not our goal at this time). Another picture shows with the initial letter sound.
- The student clicks on the x above the picture and is returned to the screen with all the letters.

Note: If you do not have access to the Internet, the Starfall group of programs can be purchased on a CD for around $20. Call customer service at 888-857-8990 or email them at learn@starfall.com and ask how to buy the Classic Starfall CD-Rom via mail.

Lesson Two: Rhymes

Recognizing rhyme is a part of phonemic awareness. It helps students pay attention to the endings of words and get the rhythm of poetry. Rhyming activities also serve as transitions to word families such as /at/, /bat/, /cat/, /sat/. For years, young children learned nursery rhymes before they began to read. Now nursery rhymes are out of fashion, and most children do not have that kind of background. However, students can still use poetry and songs to respond to rhymes. This lesson features camp songs because many older students are already aware of them, and these songs often have funny quirks to them. First, though, we teach short words that rhyme. The students should be able to tell whether or not two words rhyme. Afterwards, they should be able to identify rhymes in short songs and poems.

Objectives:
- The student will be able to tell whether one-syllable words rhyme or not.
- The student will recognize sets of rhyming words in speech, songs, and poetry.

Materials: List of possible pairs of rhymes

Success Step: Ask the student to tell you a short word that starts with /f/ or another consonant sound he knows.

Procedure:
- Tell the student to listen to these words: bat, hat, rat, sat.
- Ask him what is the same about these words. (They sound the same, they have the same end, or they rhyme.)
- Tell him examples of other rhyming pairs such as: Bug—rug; mop—top; end—bend.
- Ask the student(s) whether the following are rhyme pairs:

lad—sad	band—bank
tall—ball	am—jam
hop—pop	sing—ring
ice—sack	dip—quick
book—look	tap—stop
hill—pill	cup—gum
doll—tent	well—fell
pin—pit	shut—shoot
bun—run	same—game
	lip—dip

■ If the student answers wrong (e.g., says band and bank rhyme), tell him that those words start the same, but you want him to listen to the end of the words. (The student has already learned to hear the beginning sounds when he did the consonant sounds lessons, above.)

■ If the student does not know which are the rhyming pairs, see if he will respond to a silly chant. Tell him this chant:

Birdie, birdie in the sky.

Dropped some white wash in my eye.

Now I'm not sick and I won't cry,

But I'm just glad that cows don't fly!

■ Have him say the chant with you several times. Point out the words that rhyme.
■ Then you say the chant, leaving off the rhyming word and see if he can supply it.

Birdie, birdie in the sky.

Dropped some white wash in my _____.

Now I'm not sick and I won't _____,

But I'm just glad that cows don't _____.

■ You can help him remember the words by using gestures (point to eye, make fingers come from eyes like tears, fly with arms.)
■ Teach the rhyming songs or chants and have the students identify the rhyming words. This is intended to be a fun activity that is repeated many times. At first you may have to give a sentence at a time and ask which word rhymes with the first sentence.
■ If the student seems to understand rhyming, just review one or two of the chants or songs at the beginning of each lesson. You can laugh at the songs and chants with the students and make the lesson entertaining.

Go Fish Rhyme Game

- Cut out the cards in Appendix B2 or from the CD.
- Go through the cards with the students, explaining what word it illustrates. For example, *rat* could also be *mouse*.
- Give 5 cards to each player. You must be a player also.
- Place the rest of the cards in a pile on the table, face down.
- The first player asks the next player if he has a card that rhymes with one of the cards in his hand: "Do you have a card that rhymes with *hill?*"
- If the second player does not have a matching card, the first player takes one card from the pile.
- The next person takes his turn.
- If the second player has a matching card, he must give it to the first player. The first player then puts down the matching rhyming pair. The first player can then ask for a card to match another card in his hand.
- The player with the most rhyme pairs wins.
- The student does not match the words and pictures. He *listens* to see if someone asks for an item that rhymes with a card that he has. When the students first start the game, the teacher will have to go over each card in each student's hand so the student knows what each card represents.

(Adapted from Fish Wish game, Think Quest, TQ22 Fifth Grade Team, Canyon View Elementary School, San Diego, California)

- The *Elbow Chant* can be used at eating times so the students really know the chant well.

Elbow Chant

Joe, Joe strong and able

Get your elbows off the table

This is not a horses' stable,

But a first-class dining table.

Iggle Wiggle

(Use as many lines as you think the student can memorize)

Can you iggle, can you wiggle?

Can you jump back and giggle?

Can you rake, can you break?

Can you do the snake?

Can you tap, can you clap?

Can you sing a rap?

On Top of Spaghetti *(sung to On Top of Old Smoky)*

On top of spaghetti
All covered with cheese,
I lost my poor meatball
When somebody sneezed.
It rolled off the table
And onto the floor
And then my poor meatball
Rolled straight out the door.
Into the garden and under a bush
And then when I found it
It was nothing but mush.

Note: *You can write some of the lyrics on a board and see if the students notice that many times rhyming words are spelled with the same last letters—not always but often.*

Boom Boom, Ain't It Great to be Crazy

Way down south where bananas grow,
a flea stepped on an elephant's toe.
The elephant said with tears in his eyes,
Why don't you pick on someone your size?

Grandma's Lye Soap

(Use as many lines as seem practical)
You remember Grandma's Lye soap,
Good for everything in the home
And the secret was in the scrubbing
It wouldn't suds, and couldn't foam!

CHORUS:
Oh, let us sing of Grandma's Lye Soap
Let us sing all over the place.
The pots and pans, the dirty dishes-
And for your hands, and for your face.

Little Herman and brother Thurman
Had an aversion to washing their ears
Grandma scrubbed them with the lye soap
Now they haven't heard a word in years!

REPEAT CHORUS
Mrs. O'Talley, down in the valley
Suffered from ulcers, I understand
Swallowed a cake of Grandma's Lye Soap-
Has the cleanest ulcers in the land!

> Remember that these chants and songs have different words in different areas of the country. Girls' and boys' camps, other activity organizations, and families have learned different versions of them. You can use the words that you know—as long as they have words that rhyme.

Do Your Ears Hang Low?

(Best sung rather than chanted)
Do your ears hang low?
Do they wobble to and fro?
Can you tie 'em in a knot?
Can you tie 'em in a bow?
Can you throw 'em over your shoulder
Like a continental soldier?
Do your ears hang low?

Striped Skunk

I'm a little stripe-ed skunk
Hiding under someone's bunk.
No one wants to stay with me,
'Cause I'm as stinky as can be.

I'm a Nut

(Use as many verses as practical)
I'm a nut, big and round,
Lying on the cold, cold ground.
People come and stomp on me,
That is why, I'm cracked you see.

Chorus:
I'm a nut (clap, clap), I'm a nut (clap, clap),
I'm a nut, I'm a nut, I'm a nut (clap, clap)

Called myself, on the telephone.
Just to see if I was home.
Asked myself on a date,
Pick me up at half past eight.

Chorus:

Took myself to the picture show

Sat right down in the very third row

Wrapped my arms around my waist

Got so fresh, I slapped my face.

Evaluation:

1. Ask the student to tell which are rhyming pairs:
   - lad—bad
   - band—hand
   - pan—man
   - like—look
   - row—show

2. Ask him to tell you which words rhyme in this poem:

I'm a little pile of <u>tin</u>,

No one knows what shape I'm <u>in</u>,

Got four wheels and a running <u>board</u>

I'm a 4-door, I'm a <u>Ford</u>.

Parents and tutors can use the questions to determine whether the student understands rhymes. Teachers can write 5 -10 additional questions if they are evaluating students using curriculum-based measuring (CBM) and need to measure growth on a regular basis.

Level One Phonics

Students who are ready for Level One Phonics will know most of the letter names and some of the sounds of letters. For instance, they will know that /s/ makes the "ssss" sound or /m/ makes the "mmm" sound. In Level One, they will move on to learning all sounds of the consonants.

Letter Sounds—Consonants

Many consonants' names have the beginning of the letter sound somewhere in the name. You can make the sounds of some of the letters such as /s/,/l/,/v/, and /f/ by prolonging them as long as the breath lasts. Most people produce the sounds of the other letters by adding the vowel sound /uh/ after the beginning of the sound of the letter (stops, etc.). For example, the name of the letter B starts with the /b/ sound. By putting the vowel sound /uh/ after the /b/ sound (replacing the ee sound), the student can isolate the /b/ sound.

Some instructions for teaching reading tell parents and teachers not to include the /uh/ sound when making the letter sound. Most adults add the /uh/ sound anyway. I have not found that students have difficulty replacing the /uh/ with an appropriate ending letter.

Sometimes a student can't make the sound of the letter when asked, but she can tell you a word that starts with that letter. She probably does understand the concept even if she is unable to isolate the sound.

Lesson One: Initial Consonant Sounds

Objectives:

- The student will identify initial consonant sounds when given the words orally.
- The student will be able to produce the sounds for the consonant letters of the alphabet. Or: The student will be able to produce a word beginning with named consonants.

Materials:

- The Letter Sounds Flashcards from Appendix B3/CD, either printed out on cardstock or printed on regular paper and glued to index cards
- 3 x 5 index cards, glue, and scissors
- Black marker
- Paper and black marker (or whiteboard)

Success Step: Have the student point to some letters that you name (letters that you know that she knows).

Procedure:

- Choose four consonant letter cards to introduce to the student (possibly M, S, P, T).
- Start with a sound that can be extended and emphasized for the student to hear the sound. For example, /s/ can be prolonged as sssss.
- Ask the student what letter is on the first card.
- Student: /S/
- Teacher: "Yes, the name of the letter is /S/, but the letter also has a sound: /ssss/. The key word is *sun*. The first sound in the word *sun* starts with /sss/. Repeat the sound /sss/ with me."
- Ask the student what letter is on the second card.
- Student: P

Starfall Activity

Use the website Starfall to continue learning letter sounds.

- Load the program Starfall from the Internet: www.starfall.com.
- Bring up the #1 Starfall program—"ABCs: Let's Get Ready to Read." Click to bring up the screen with all the letters.
- Click on one of the consonant letters you have taught the student.
- The program shows the capital letter and the lower case letter and names them. (The student has previously used this program to learn the letter names.)
- The student clicks the arrow below the picture. The program then gives the letter sound. This is our goal now. Another picture shows with the initial letter sound.
- Have the student repeat the letter sound.
- The student then clicks on the x above the picture and is returned to the screen with all the letters and chooses another of her consonant sounds.

- Teacher: "Yes, the name of this letter is p, but the letter also has a sound: /puh/. The key word is *pig*. The first sound in *pig* is the /puh/ sound. Repeat that sound with me."
- Write the two letters on a piece of paper or a whiteboard: S   P
- Have the student match the flashcard consonant cards to the letters written on the board or paper.
- Repeat the above procedure with another two flashcard consonant cards that the student does not know.
- Write all four consonants on the board or paper and have the student match the flashcards to the letters.
- Have the student practice with the flashcard consonant cards.
- Have the student name words that start with those letter sounds.
- You must repeat these procedures over and over again so the student can make the initial SOUND of the consonants or identify a word starting with that SOUND.

Activities/Games

Tower Game

Play the Tower Game to reinforce knowledge of letter sounds at the beginning words.

- Cut out two towers (for each player) from Appendix B4/CD.
- Cut out the cards to be put on the floors of the towers from the Appendix or the CD.
- Put a key word for a consonant on the roof of each tower. Review the word for each picture; e.g., *pig* or *hog*.

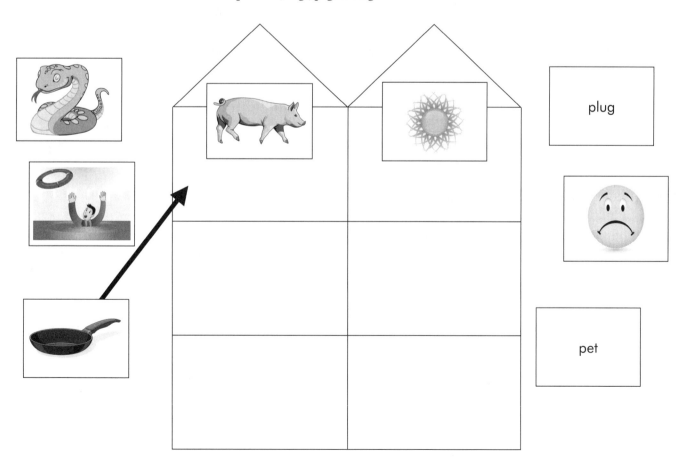

- Put the flashcards in a pile with word or picture showing.
- The student takes the first card, makes the appropriate sound and places it on the floor of the matching tower.
- The players take turns placing the cards on the floor of the towers.
- The first student (or adult) to completely fill all the floors of one tower is the winner.
- Play the Tower Game with all the consonant sounds the student needs to learn. Change the picture at the top of each tower as you change the consonant she will be learning. Use the Letter Sounds Flashcards (Appendix B3) for the new picture on the Tower top. Make at least three word cards for each consonant the student needs to learn. There are blank boxes for additional pictures or words that you may need in the Appendix B4.

Hints for Teaching Letter Sounds

These optional strategies are designed for students who need multisensory cues to memorize the letters.

- Have the students trace or produce the letters on lined paper.
- Have the students write the letters with one finger on their desk.
- Use gestural cues:

  P = Open and close fists as if popping
  M = Rub stomach as if liking food ("mmmm")
  J = Jump
  T = "Tick, tock" while pointing to watch
  U = Point up
  S = "Ssss" while making snake with finger
  B = Make a ball with hands
  Z = Buzzing bee
  N = Shake head for no
  H = Pant as if out of breath
  V = "Vvvvroom" as if motor
  C = Cup one hand (other sound of /c/ given later)

Lesson Two: Consonant Digraphs (H–Words)

A consonant digraph is made from two consonants that join together to produce a single sound. Students need to learn the sounds of digraphs because many of the words used for beginning reading contain wh, th, sh, ch, and ph.

Objective: The student will be able to decode words using consonant digraphs (H words: sh, wh, ch, and th).

Materials:

- Flashcards made by cutting 3 x 5 index cards in half and then writing the letters w, s, c, t, h, h, h, h on the half-sized cards.
- Black marker
- Words with and without digraphs cut from the boxes in the Appendix B5/CD

- Cube Game with Digraphs copied onto cardstock or used file folders from Appendix B5/CD
- Transparent tape

Success Step: Have the student identify the letters /w/, /s/, /c/, /t/, and /h/ from flashcards.

Procedure:

- Show the students the flashcards from the success step on the table. Tell the students that adding an /h/ to each of these letters makes a completely different sound. These two letters make one sound.
- Start with the letters /c/ and /h/. Tell your student(s) the sound of /ch/, relating it to the sound of "ah-choo" when sneezing.
- Have the students pronounce the /ch/ sound several times.
- Tell them that the /ch/ sound can also come at the end of a word. Example: teach, beach.
- Slowly read the following list of words to the students. Say each word twice. If the /ch/ is in the word, the students should say "ah-choo." If the /ch/ is not in the word, the students should be silent or say "no."

a. Cherry	e. Light	h. Ouch
b. Beach	f. Chalk	i. Touch
c. White	g. Red	j. Mat
d. Chip		

- Repeat the above procedure with /t/ and /h/. Show the students the tongue position for /th/. Have them practice the /th/ sound.
- Slowly read a list of the following words to the students. Say each word twice. If the /th/ is in the word, the students should say "tongue out." If the /th/ is not in the word, the students should be silent or say no.

a. They	e. There	h. With
b. Tree	f. Thumbs	i. Heat
c. Thing	g. Fish	j. Their
d. Dream		

- Use the computer program Starfall, if appropriate.

Practicing Digraphs /ch/ and /th/ with Starfall

- Log onto the Starfall website: www.starfall.com.
- Bring up the "Learn to Read" program, then the Skills section of Unit 8 for digraph ch.
- The program will pronounce /ch/ several times and then present words with /ch/. This section has a choo-choo train as a symbol, which may not be age-appropriate for your student(s). You can tell the student ahead of time that the program has a choo-choo train for younger students. Remind her that older students like her use a sneeze (ah-choo) instead.
- The student needs to click on the /ch/ of each word that is presented.
- Then go to the Skills section of Unit 7 for digraph /th/.
- The program will pronounce /th/ several times and then present words with /th/.
- The student needs to click on the /th/ of each word that is presented.

- Repeat the above procedure with /w/ and /h/. Show the students the wind sound (blowing a candle out) for /wh/ digraph. The *wh/* digraph varies in pronunciation from word to word and from dialect to dialect. Most often it sounds like the /w/ as in *whale,* or sometimes like the /h/ sound as in *whole.* Many interrogative words begin with /wh/, so this sound should be addressed.
- Slowly read a list of the following words to the students. Name each word twice. If the /wh/ is in the word, the students should make the wind sound. If the /wh/ is not in the word, the students should be silent or say "no."

a. White	e. Look	h. Hot
b. What	f. Wheel	i. Whistle
c. Why	g. Gate	j. Ham
d. Link		

- Then tell the students that when h is added to s, it becomes a new sound: /sh/, like the sound you make when you want someone to be quiet. You can make a sign for /sh/ by putting your pointer finger in front of your mouth as if signaling for quiet.
- Slowly read a list of the following words to the students. Say each word twice. If the /sh/ is in the word, the students should make the shhh sound. If the /sh/ is not in the word, the students should be silent or say "no."

a. Shop	e. Chap	i. Bus
b. Wash	f. Shine	j. Drink
c. Shell	g. Dish	k. Sad
d. Shut	h. Shower	

- Use the website Starfall, if appropriate.

Practicing Digraphs wh and sh with Starfall

- Log on to the Starfall website on the computer: www.starfall.com.
- Bring up the "Learn to Read" program, then the Skills section of Unit 6 for digraph wh.
- The program will pronounce /wh/ several times and then present words with /wh/. The student needs to click on the /wh/ of each word that is presented.
- Then go to the Skills section of Unit 4 for digraph /sh/.
- The program will pronounce /sh/ several times and then present words with /sh/.
- The student needs to click on the /sh/ of each word that is presented.

Activity/Game

Cube Game with Digraphs

- Cut out the cube in Appendix B5 or print out from the CD. Use transparent tape to tape the figure into a cube.

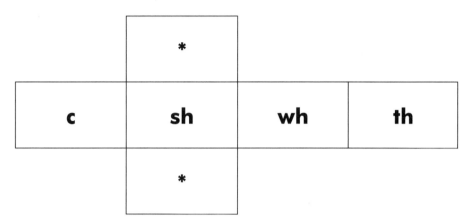

- Cut out the word cards using or not using digraphs (also in Appendix B5/CD) and spread them out in front of the students.
- Using the cube like a die, have one student shake and toss the cube. If the cube lands with a digraph sh on top, the student should find a word card that has an /sh/ in it. If she is correct, she gets to keep that word card. The digraph may begin or end the word.
- If the cube lands with a star on top, she must choose a word that does not have a digraph in it. If she is correct, she also gets to keep the word card.
- The students (or teacher and student) should take turns tossing the cube.
- If an appropriate word card is not available, the other student (or teacher) takes the next turn.
- The winner is the one with the most word cards when all the word cards have been taken. The teacher or tutor may set a time limit on the game and set a timer, if time is limited.

Generalization Activities

1. Go to the Language Experience stories the student has written with you. Have the student find the words that start with the consonants she has been studying. Have her read the words and isolate the letter sound (if possible).
2. If the student's stories do not include appropriate words, make up some sentences with words starting with the needed consonants for her to read. She does not need to be able to read the rest of the sentence. For example:

Show me where the whale threw the chocolate bar.

It is essential to show the student that the lessons she is learning have an important purpose. It is even more important to try to use the student's own words to illustrate that purpose.

Short Vowels

The student should memorize those letters that are vowels. "A, E, I, O, U" are usually taught in sort of a sing-song chant. Vowels usually have two or more possible sounds. Each syllable in English includes one or more vowels, but vowels are often in the middle of words, which makes them more difficult to hear. Long vowels are the same as the alphabet names of the letters, so they are easier to learn as a group. However, short vowels are used more frequently in the short words or syllables that students first learn. Many students are able to learn the vowel sounds by chanting the letter name, a word starting with the short vowel, and then the short vowel sound:

Vowels

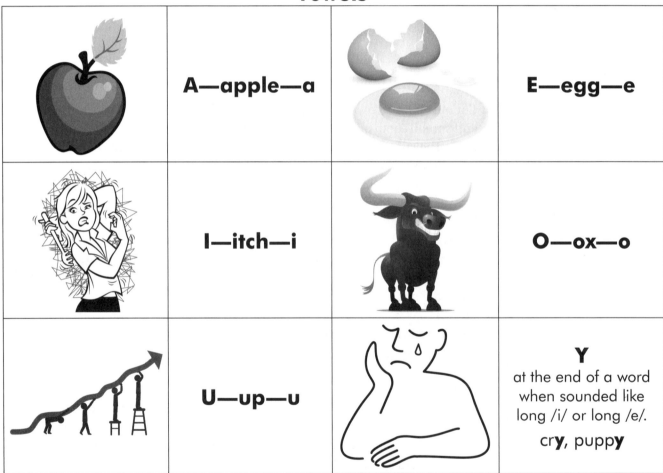

	A—apple—a		E—egg—e
	I—itch—i		O—ox—o
	U—up—u		**Y** at the end of a word when sounded like long /i/ or long /e/. cr**y**, pupp**y**

Note: say, "For Y at the end when it says eye or ee."

Some students have difficulty reproducing the short vowel sounds by themselves. However, researchers have found that vowels are easier to learn as part of a word with meaning. Short words are divided into the letters before the vowel (the onset) and the rime, which includes the vowel(s) and the consonants that follow. For example, *hat* is divided into the onset /h/ and the rime /at/. *Cat, hat, rat,* and *fat* are a family of words with the /at/ as the rime at the end. These word family patterns help students learn many other words.

Lesson Three: Short /a/ Sound

This lesson is taught mainly with words that follow a syllable pattern of consonant-vowel-consonant (CVC).

Objective: The student will recognize the short /a/ in words and produce the word families /at/, /an/, /ak/, and /ap/.

Materials:

- Cut out the vowel flashcards (shown on the bottom of the Letter Sounds Flashcards (Appendix B3 or CD) and show the appropriate card as you teach the short vowels.
- Word Family Worksheets with Crazy Rhymes and short a words (from Appendix B6 or CD); enough for each student to have a copy
- Lined paper and pencil
- Scrabble game, with the letters divided into vowels and consonants and placed in plastic bags

Success Step: Have the student name the vowels.

Procedure:

- Use the /a/ flashcard and say the phrase: **A, apple, /a/.** Explain that you name the capital letter, say the short word beginning with that letter, and then isolate that short beginning sound. (Don't talk with the student about contrasting the long and short vowel sound until you finish all the short vowels.)

- Have the student repeat the phrase at least 3 times.
- Say the short sound of "a" at least 2 times.
- Have the student repeat the above at the beginning of each session with short /a/.

Word Family /ap/

- Pronounce the rime /ap/ to the student by saying it several times. Tell her that she is learning parts of words to help her in reading. We call these parts of words "word families."
- Have the student repeat the rime.
- Tell the student the Crazy Rhyme for /ap/, /an/, and/or /at/ and do the activities for that rhyme. (Depending on the student's interests and abilities, you might cover one or more rhymes per day. However, you want to review the Crazy Rhymes at the beginning of several sessions.)

Crazy Rhyme (using /ap/)

> **My name is Zap.**
>
> **I fell into a trap.**
>
> **I lost my cap.**
>
> **Guess I will take a nap.**

- Have the student chant the rhyme frequently and memorize, if possible.
- Copy Word Family Worksheet/Crazy Rhyme for /ap/ from Appendix B6 or print it out from the CD. Have the student circle the /ap/s in the Crazy Rhyme and the listed words. Have the student read the /ap/ words.
- Have the student handwrite the Crazy Rhyme and the /ap/ words on lined paper and underline the /ap/ rime.

Word Family /an/

- Pronounce the rime /an/ to the student by saying it several times.
- Have the student repeat the rime.
- Tell the student the Crazy Rhyme for /an/.

Crazy Rhyme (using /an/)

> **I look for my lizard Dan,**
>
> **Is he under the can?**
>
> **Is he under the pan?**
>
> **No, away he ran.**

- Chant the rhyme frequently and memorize, if possible.
- Copy the /an/ worksheet/Crazy Rhyme from Appendix B6 (or print it out from the CD) and have the student circle the /an/ in the Crazy Rhyme and the listed words. Have the student read the /an/ words.
- Have the student handwrite the Crazy Rhyme and the /an/ words on lined paper and underline the /an/ rime.
- Pronounce the rime /at/ to the student by saying it several times.
- Have the student repeat the rhyme.

Word Family /at/

■ Tell the student the Crazy Rhyme for /at/.

Crazy Rhyme (using /at/)

Hey Pat,

You sat

On my hat,

Don't do that!

You'll get hit with a bat.

■ Have the student chant the rhyme frequently and memorize, if possible.
■ Copy the /at/ worksheet from Appendix B6 (or print it out from the CD) and have the student circle the /at/s in the Crazy Rhyme and the listed words. Have the student read the /at/ words.
■ Have the student write the Crazy Rhyme and the /at/ words on lined paper and underline the /at/ rime.

Activities/Games

Scrabble Words

■ Take out the plastic or wooden letters from the Scrabble game. Separate them into vowels and consonants, if you haven't already done so.
■ Tape together the letters /a/ and /p/, /a/ and /t/, and /a/ and /n/. Use clear tape that can be removed later.

A	P		A	T		A	N

■ Put some of the consonant tiles from the Scrabble game on the table in front of the students, letter side up.
■ Take turns making words with the consonants attached to the word families you have taped together.

C	A	P

■ Each student receives 2 points for every correct word she makes. If the student makes a nonsense word, she can get 1 point if she pronounces it correctly.
■ The student or teacher with the most points when time is up is the winner.
■ You can determine how much time to allow for this activity/game.
■ Later you can put the consonant Scrabble letters with the letter-side down so there is more chance involved in the game.

Starfall

Short /a/ is covered by the website Starfall. The Starfall program makes phonics learning interesting. You do not have to use Starfall. However, I have found that most secondary students do not consider the graphics of Starfall babyish, and they certainly are interested in using the computer. You can, however, teach the phonics lessons using just the materials in this book.

- Go to the Starfall website: www.starfall.com.
- Bring up the #2 Starfall program – "Learn to Read: Zac the Rat and Other Tales," and click on "Line One – Play."

- The Play program shows four possible initial letters, a picture such as a fan, and the word without the initial letter. The student moves the correct letter with the computer mouse to the right place in the word. The student can click on any word and have it pronounced for her.

F

C

P

R

__an

- Next an illustrated short story is shown using the short /a/ as in ap, at, and an. Included are some sight words that can be pre-taught. The student stops on each word and reads it aloud. If she does not know the word, she clicks on that word, and it is pronounced for her. The objective is for the student to read the sentences fluently with no mistakes. It may take many readings to accomplish this objective, but the format of the unit is similar to video games, and students usually enjoy it.

Generalization Activities

1. Refer to the language experience stories you have written with the student. Have the student find any words that have a short /a/ in them. Do the same with the structured reading stories by other authors in Part III, if your student is working with those stories.
2. If these stories do not contain enough short /a/ words, write several sentences containing short /a/ words. Example:

Tad can bat a ball at the fat cat.

It is important that the students see that the phonics they are learning can be applied to real reading.

Evaluation: Have the student read the following words:

1. can	5. tap	8. pan
2. ran	6. bat	9. rap
3. at	7. fat	10. nap
4. man		

The student should be able to read 90% of the words. Do not count a word as incorrect if the student has not learned the onset letter.

Lesson Four: Short /i/ Sound

This lesson is taught mainly using words that follow a syllable pattern of consonant-vowel-consonant (CVC).

Objective: The student will recognize the short /i/ in words and produce the word families /ip/, /it/, and /ig/.

Materials:

- Flashcard of the vowel /i/ from Appendix B3 or CD
- Word Family Worksheets with Crazy Rhymes and short /i/ words from Appendix B6 or CD
- Lined paper and pencil
- Scrabble letters divided into vowels and consonants, in clear plastic bags

Success Step: Have the student name an /a/ word taught in the previous section.

Procedures:

- Use the /i/ flash card and say the phrase: **I—itch—/i/**. Say: I (eye), itch, i (with a short sound).

- Have the student repeat the phrase at least 3 times.
- Say the short sound of /i/ at least 2 times.
- Have the student repeat the above at the beginning of each session with short /i/.
- You may teach the student the gesture of itching to remember the short i sound.

Word Family /it/

- Pronounce the rime /it/ to the student by saying it several times.
- Have the student repeat the rime.
- Tell the student the Crazy Rhyme for /it/.

Crazy Rhyme (using /it/)

Buying Shoes

Will it fit?

Just a bit?

If I sit?

Oh, I quit!

- Have the student chant the rhyme frequently and memorize, if possible.
- Copy the Word Family Worksheet (Crazy Rhyme) for /it/ from Appendix B6 (or print it out from the CD) and have the student circle the /it/s in the Crazy Rhyme and the listed words. Have the student read the /it/ words.
- Have the student write the /it/ rhyme and the /it/ words on lined paper and circle the /it/s.

Word Family /ip/

- Pronounce the rime /ip/ to the student by saying it several times.
- Have the student repeat the rime.
- Tell the student the Crazy Rhyme for /ip/.

Crazy Rhyme (using /ip/)

I dip,

I flip,

I slip.

What a trip!

- Chant the rhyme frequently and memorize, if possible.
- Copy the worksheet for /ip/ from Appendix B6 (or print it out from CD) and have the student circle the /ip/s in the Crazy Rhyme and the listed words. Have the student read the /ip/ words.
- Have the student write the Crazy Rhyme and the /ip/ words on lined paper and circle the /ip/ rime.

Word Family /ig/

- Pronounce the rime /ig/ to the student by saying it several times.
- Have the student repeat the rime.
- Tell the student the Crazy Rhyme for /ig/.

Crazy Rhyme (using /ig/)

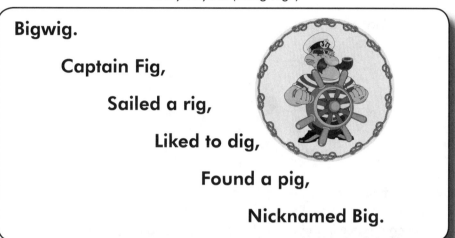

Bigwig.

Captain Fig,

Sailed a rig,

Liked to dig,

Found a pig,

Nicknamed Big.

- Have the student chant the rhyme frequently and memorize, if possible.
- Copy the Word Family Worksheet and Crazy Rhyme from Appendix B6 (or print it out from the CD) and have the student circle the /ig/s in the Crazy Rhyme and the listed words. Have the student read the /ig/ words.
- Have the student write the Crazy Rhyme and the /ig/ words on lined paper and circle the /ig/ rime.

Activity/Game

Scrabble Words

- Tape together the plastic or wooden Scrabble letters /i/ and / t/, /i/ and /p/, and /i/ and /g/. Use clear tape that can be removed later.

| I | T | | I | P | | I | G |

- Put the consonant letters on the table in front of the students – letter side up.
- Take turns making words with the consonants on the table.

| P | I | G |

- Each student receives 2 points for every correct word. If the student makes a nonsense word, she can get 1 point if she pronounces if correctly.
- The student or teacher with the most points when time is up is the winner.
- You can determine how much time to allow for this activity/game.

- Later you can put the consonant letters face-down so there is more of an element of chance in what words the students can make.

Starfall

- Go to the Starfall website: www.starfall.com.
- Bring up the #2 Starfall program – "Learn to Read: Zac the Rat and Other Tales," and click on Unit 3 – "The Big Hit—Play."

- The Play program shows four possible initial letters, a picture such as a pig, and the word without the initial letter. The student moves the correct letter with the computer mouse to the right place in the word. The student can click on any word and have it pronounced for her.

D

B

W

P   **_ig**

- Next an illustrated short story is shown using the short /i/ as in /it/, /ig/, and /ip/. Included are some sight words that can be pre-taught. The student stops on each word and reads it aloud. If she does not know the word, she clicks on that word, and it is pronounced for her. The objective is for the student to read the sentences fluently with no mistakes. It may take many readings to accomplish this objective, but the format of the unit is similar to video games, and students usually enjoy it.

Generalization Activities

1. Refer to the language experience stories you have written with the student. Have the student find any words that have a short /i/ in them. Do the same with the structured reading stories that are provided in Part 3 if the student is doing those parts. It is important that the students see that the phonics lessons can be applied to real reading.
2. You can also write several sentences that have words containing short /i/. Example:

Kit hit the pig with the pin.

Evaluation: Have the student read the following words. The student should be able to read 90% of the words. Do not count words as incorrect if the student has not learned the onset letter.

1. tip
2. rip
3. wig
4. zip

5. big
6. hit
7. bit

8. dip
9. mitt
10. gig

Lesson Five: Short o and Short u Families

There aren't as many word families that use short o or short u as there are word families that use short /a/, /e/, and /i/, so I have combined the /o/ and /u/ exercises.

The Short /o/ Sound

Objective: The student will recognize the short /o/ in words and produce the word families /op/, /ot/ and /og/.

Materials:

- Flashcard of the vowel /o/ from Appendix B3 or CD.
- Word Family Sheets (Crazy Rhymes) for short /o/ words (Appendix B6)
- Lined paper and pencil
- Plastic or wooden letters from a Scrabble game divided into vowels and consonants – in plastic bags

Success Step: Have the student name an /i/ word taught in the previous section.

Procedures:

- Use the /o/ flashcard and say the phrase: O – ox—/o/

O — ox — /o/

- Have the student repeat the phrase at least 3 times.
- Say the short sound of /o/ at least 2 times.
- You may teach the student the gesture of a doctor having someone say "ah" to remember the short o sound.
- Pronounce the rime /op/ to the student by saying it several times.
- Have the student repeat the rime.

Word Family /op/ and /ot/

- Pronounce the rime /ot/ to the student.
- Tell her that she is going to learn two rimes in this lesson, /op/ and /ot/.
- Pronounce the rimes /ot/ and /op/ to the student by saying them several times.
- Tell the student the Crazy Rhyme for /op/and /ot/.

Crazy Rhyme (using /op/ and /ot/)

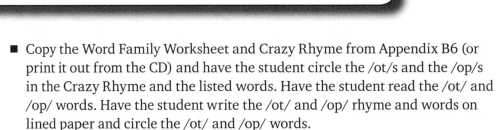

Scott got a pot.

The soup was hot.

He spilled a lot.

Here comes Pop.

He brings a mop.

- Copy the Word Family Worksheet and Crazy Rhyme from Appendix B6 (or print it out from the CD) and have the student circle the /ot/s and the /op/s in the Crazy Rhyme and the listed words. Have the student read the /ot/ and /op/ words. Have the student write the /ot/ and /op/ rhyme and words on lined paper and circle the /ot/ and /op/ words.

The Short /u/ Sound

Objective: The student will recognize the short /u/ in words and produce the word families /up/ and /ug/.

Materials:

- Flashcard of the vowel /u/ from Appendix B3 or CD
- Word Family Worksheet (Crazy Rhymes) for short /u/ words from Appendix B6
- Lined paper and pencil
- Scrabble letters divided into vowels and consonants – in plastic bags

Procedures:

- Use the /u/ flashcard and say the phrase: U – up—/u/

U — up — /u/

- Have the student repeat the phrase at least 3 times.
- Say the short sound of /u/ at least 2 times.
- Have the student repeat the above at the beginning of each session with short /u/.
- You may teach the student the gesture of pointing up to remember the short u sound.

Word Family /ug/ and /ub/

- Tell the student the Crazy Rhyme for /ug/and /ub/.

Crazy Rhyme (using /ug/ and /ub/)

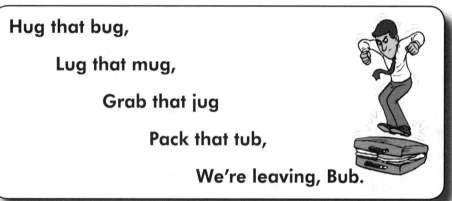

Hug that bug,

Lug that mug,

Grab that jug

Pack that tub,

We're leaving, Bub.

- Chant the rhyme frequently and memorize, if possible.
- Copy the Word Family Worksheet (Crazy Rhyme) from the Appendix (or print it out from the CD) and have the student circle the /ug/s and /ub/s in the Crazy Rhyme and the listed words. Have the student read the /u/ words.
- Have the student write the Crazy Rhyme and the /u/ words on lined paper and circle the /ub/ and /ug/ rimes.

Activity/Game

Scrabble Words

- Tape together the following pairs of plastic or wooden letters from a Scrabble game: /o/ and /t/, /o/ and /p/, /u/ and /b/, and /u/ and /g/. Use clear tape that can be removed later.

| O | T | | O | P | | U | B | | U | G |

- Put the Scrabble consonant letters on the table in front of the students, letter side up.
- Take turns making words with the consonants on the table.

| B | U | G |

- Each student receives 2 points for every correct word. If the student makes a nonsense word, she can get 1 point if she pronounces it correctly.
- The student or teacher with the most points when time is up is the winner.
- You can determine how much time to allow for this activity/game.
- Later you can put the consonants letter-side down so the students have more of an element of chance in what words they can make.

Starfall

- Log onto the Starfall website: www.starfall.com.
- Bring up the #2 Starfall program – "Learn to Read: Zac the Rat and Other Tales," and click on Unit 4 – "Mox's Shop" or Unit 5 – "Gus the Duck"—Play.
- The Play program shows four possible initial letters, a picture such as a hog, and the word without the initial letter. The student moves the correct letter with the computer mouse to the right place in the word. The student can click on any word and have it pronounced for her.
- Next, an illustrated short story is shown using the short o. Included are some sight words that can be pre-taught. The student stops on each word and reads it aloud. If she does not know the word, she clicks on that word, and it is pronounced for her. The objective is for the student to read the sentences fluently with no mistakes.

Generalization Activities

1. Refer to the language experience stories you have written with the student. Have the student find any words that have a short /o/ or short /u/ in them. Do the same with the structured reading stories that are provided in Part 3. It is important for students to see that phonics can be applied to real reading.
2. You may want to write several sentences for the student using short /u/ and short /o/. Examples:

Bob has a dog named Hot Dog.

The bus was full of mud and gum.

Evaluation: Have the student read the words in the following list. The student should be able to read 90% of the words. Do not count a word as incorrect if the student has not learned the beginning letter.

1. bug	5. dot	8. flub
2. tub	6. top	9. sub
3. snug	7. mug	10. mop
4. stop		

Lesson Six: The Short /e/ Sound

Objective: The student will recognize the short /e/ in words and produce the word families /en/, /et/, and /ell/.

Materials:

- Flashcard of the vowel /e/ from Appendix B3/CD
- Word Family Worksheets of Crazy Rhymes and short /e/ words from Appendix B6
- Lined paper and pencil
- Plastic or wooden letters from a Scrabble game divided into vowels and consonants – in plastic bags

Success Step: Have the student name an /o/ or /u/ word taught in the previous section.

Procedures:

- Use the /e/ flashcard and say the phrase: E—**egg**—/e/

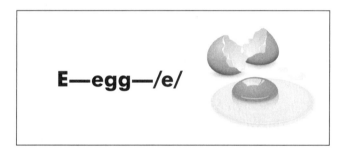

- Have the student repeat the phrase at least 3 times.
- Say the short sound of /e/ at least 2 times.
- Have the student repeat the above at the beginning of each session with short /e/.
- You may teach the student the gesture of breaking an egg to remember the short /e/ sound.
- Next you will be teaching the word family /en/.

Word Family /en/

- Say the rime /en/ to the student several times.
- Have the student repeat the rime.
- Tell the student the Crazy Rhyme for /en/.

Crazy Rhyme (using /en/)

When I count to ten,

My hen named Jen

Crows Amen.

- Have the student chant the rhyme frequently and memorize, if possible.
- Copy the Word Family Worksheet and Crazy Rhyme from Appendix B6 (or print it out from the CD) and have the student circle the /en/s in the Crazy Rhyme and the listed words. Have the student read the /en/ words. Have the student write the /en/ rhyme and the /en/ words on lined paper and circle the /en/s.

Word Family /et/

- Say the rime /et/ to the student several times.
- Have the student repeat the rime.
- Tell the student the Crazy Rhyme for /et/.

Crazy Rhyme (using /et/)

I bet,

You'll get wet,

My water cannon shoots a jet.

- Chant the rhyme frequently and memorize, if possible.
- Copy the Word Family Worksheet and Crazy Rhyme from Appendix B6 (or print it out from the CD) and have the student circle the /et/s in the Crazy Rhyme and the listed words. Have the student read the /et/ words.
- Have the student write the Crazy Rhyme and the /et/ words on lined paper and circle the /et/ rime.

Word Family /ell/

- Pronounce the rime /ell/ to the student by saying it several times.
- Have the student repeat the rime.
- Tell the student the Crazy Rhyme for /ell/.

Crazy Rhyme (using /ell/)

I can tell,

I can yell,

I can ring a bell.

Get rid of that smell!

- Have the student chant the rhyme frequently and memorize, if possible.

- Copy the Word Family Worksheet and Crazy Rhyme from Appendix B6 (or print it out from the CD) and have the student circle the /ell/s in the Crazy Rhyme and the listed words. Have the student read the /ell/ words.

Activity/Game

Scrabble Words

- Tape together the following pairs of plastic or wooden Scrabble letters: /e/ and /t/, /e/ and /n/, and /e/ and /l/ and /l/. Use clear tape that can be removed later.

- Put the consonant letters on the table in front of the students, letter side up.
- Take turns making words with the consonants on the table.

- Each student receives 2 points for every correct word. If the student makes a nonsense word, she can get 1 point if she pronounces if correctly.
- The student or teacher with the most points when time is up is the winner.
- You can determine how much time to allow for this activity/game.
- Later you can put the letters facedown so there is more of an element of chance in what words the students can make.

Generalization Activities

Refer to the language experience stories you have written with the student. Have the student find any words that have a short /e/ in them. Do the same with the structured reading stories that are provided in Part 3. It is important that the students see that phonics can be applied to real reading.

If you don't have enough words using short /e/, write a few sentences containing short /e/ words. Example:

Ted fed a red apple to his little pet.

Evaluation: Have the student read the words in the following list. The student should be able to read 90% of the words. Do not count a word as incorrect if the student has not learned the onset letter.

1. set
2. let
3. shell
4. when
5. amen
6. pen
7. yet
8. bell
9. hen
10. smell

Starfall

- Log onto the Starfall website: www.starfall.com.
- Bring up the #2 Starfall program – "Learn to Read: Zac the Rat and Other Tales," and click on Unit 2 – "Peg the Hen"—Play.
- The Play program shows four possible initial letters, a picture such as a jet, and the word without the initial letter. The student moves the correct letter with the computer mouse to the right place in the word. The student can click on any word and have it pronounced for her.

P

J

W

N   **__et**

- Next, an illustrated short story is shown using the short "e" as in /et/, /en/, and /ell/. Included are some sight words that can be pre-taught. The student stops on each word and reads it aloud. If she does not know the word, she clicks on that word, and it is pronounced for her. The objective is for the student to read the sentences fluently with no mistakes. It may take many readings to accomplish this objective, but the format of the unit is similar to video games, and students usually enjoy it.

Level Two Phonics

Long Vowels

Vowels in the English language have more than one sound. Level One provided lessons on the short form of the vowels because the types of words that beginning readers encounter most often have short vowel sounds. Level Two focuses on the long sounds of vowels in certain patterns.

The long sounds of the vowels are simply the alphabet names of those vowels. You can have the students name those vowels and tell them that they now know the long sounds of all the vowels. However, what is most important for them to know is when to use the long sounds. This involves learning the phonics rules for forming the long vowel sounds so that they can use them automatically. No, we do not mean that students should be able to recite the rules, but that they should be able to use the rules as they are decoding a new word.

Lesson One: Silent E

Objective: The student will recognize the silent e at the end of a word or syllable and decode the word with a long vowel.

Materials:

- Plastic or wooden letters from a Scrabble game
- Small slate board or whiteboard
- Chalk or marker (for above)
- Copies of Changing the Story from Appendix B7 or CD
- Silent E mini worksheet (in text) on board or copied on paper
- Cards for Silent E Bingo Game and Bingo list from Appendix B8 or CD

- Bingo chips (If possible, magnetic bingo wand and chips from Internet or game store, $5 -$8)

Success Step: Ask the student to tell you the long sound of /a/ and /i/. If incorrect, have him repeat the sounds after your model.

Procedures:

- Write the words *cap, kit,* and *rob* on the board. Have the student read the three words.
- Tell the student that you can change all three into different words with one stroke. Put an /e/ after *cap,* turning it into *cape.* Pronounce the word *cape.* Point out that the /e/ is silent. Erase the /e/ and let the student make *cap* into *cape.*
- Ask the student what happens when you put a silent e after *kit* and *rob.* Pronounce the words *kite* and *robe.*
- Tell the student(s) the rhyme for silent e:

Silent e—It takes the blame.
It makes the vowel say its name.

- Have the student repeat the rhyme until it is memorized.
- Point out that the rule applies to words that have a vowel-consonant and an /e/ at the end.
- Repeat the rhyme at the beginning of the next 3–5 lessons.
- Using the Scrabble pieces, make short-vowel words such as cap, pin, cub, rub, and hat. Have the student add e to each of the words and pronounce the new words. If you have more than one student, have them prepare words for each other.
- Have the student do the mini-worksheet on silent e. Have the student cross out the /e/ and put a long mark over the vowel. Explain to him that he will see the long mark in dictionaries, but won't ordinarily use it for spelling words.

Mini-worksheet on Silent e

Mark the following words by crossing out the silent e and putting a long mark over the long vowel as shown in the example.

Example: tāp̶e̶

bite   time   cane

tape   fine   made

Activities/Games

Changing the Story

- Give the student a copy of the story below from Appendix B7 or CD. Read the story out loud with the student. Have the student cross out the silent /e/ in all the words. Then you (or you and the student) read the story again. Each time you reach a word with the silent e crossed out, have the student read the word that results. The result will probably be funny, but the point will be made.

> My friend **Pete** and I made a trip to the **lake**. We sailed on **Cane Lake** in an inner **tube**. We fished. I got a **bite** with my fishing **pole**. The fish got away. That was **fine** with me. The sun started to **fade** from the sky. We saw a **huge** black cloud. It started to rain. **Pete** said, "Hey, **dude**. Do you want to **wade**?" We hurried **home**. I **hope** I get to go fishing again—but not in the rain!

Bingo Game with Silent e

- The teacher will need to play if there is only one student. Distribute the bingo cards (from Appendix B8/CD).
- Using the randomized bingo list, call out the words (most have long vowels, but some distracter words have short vowels).
- Cover the word with the bingo chip if it is on the sheet. Bingo is called when a player covers a whole line or diagonal line.
- Check the card to make sure the words are correct.

Starfall

- Log on to Starfall on the Internet: www.starfall.com.
- Bring up the #2 Starfall program—"Learn to Read."
- Click on "Unit 6—Play."
- The Play program has the student first make a short-vowel word and then add the silent e to make the long-vowel word. Next, the student clicks on a long-vowel word to color part of a picture. Parts of the picture then move.
- The following story, "Jake's Tale," uses words with a long /a/ vowel and a silent e. The student reads the words of the story out loud. The student can click on any word to hear it pronounced correctly. Starfall has stories on silent e for the following long vowels:
  - ➤ Unit 8 has material on long /i/, including a story, "Sky Ride."
  - ➤ Unit 9 has a Play section on long /o/ and also a story, "Robot and Mr. Mole."
  - ➤ Unit 10 has a Play section and a story, "Dune Buggy," which teaches long /u/. Unit 10 also has a match game with pictures and long-vowel words.
- Use these sections for additional practice on silent e. Have the student practice with these additional Play stories until he can do them fluently.

Note: Starfall has more material on long vowels and silent e than this book does. You can visit the Starfall website for additional practice and go on to other phonics principles in Level Two when the student is ready.

Evaluation: Have the student read the following words:

1. Cake	5. Ride	8. Dime
2. Ice	6. Bile	9. Fire
3. Gate	7. June	10. Life
4. Bake		

The student should be able to read 90 percent of the words. If he recognizes that the vowel becomes long when there is a silent e at the end of the word, he is considered correct—even if he does not get the rest of the word right. Give him the correct pronunciation afterward. If he scores less than 90 percent, continue working on silent e.

Lesson Two: Two Vowels Together

Objective: The student will recognize vowel pairs in the beginning or the middle of a syllable and decode the word with the sound of the first long vowel.

Materials:

- Plastic or wooden letters from a Scrabble game, divided into vowels and consonants (in plastic or fabric bags)
- Vowel Pairs Worksheet (Appendix B9 or print from CD)
- Cards for Bing-o for Vowel Pairs (Appendix B10 or print from CD)
- Bingo chips (magnetic bingo wand and chips from Internet or game store, $5 -$8)

Success Step: Ask the student to tell you the long sounds of all the vowels. If incorrect, have him repeat the sounds after your model.

Procedures:

1. Review the silent e rule for long vowel sounds. Use the word *cake* as an illustration. Show the student that the word *cake* has a consonant, then a vowel, followed by another consonant and then an *e* at the end. The student should be able to point out that the vowel /a/ says its own name in the word *cake*.
2. Tell the student that you have another way to make the vowel say its own name—if two vowels are together in the beginning or the middle of the word, the first vowel says its name, as in the word *rain*.
3. Tell the student(s) the rhyme for vowel pairs:

When two vowels go walking, the first one *usually* does the talking. (It says its own alphabet name.)

4. Have the student repeat the rhyme until it is memorized.
5. Point out that the rule applies to most words that have two vowels together, but some frequently used words are different ("outlaws")—for example, the word *said*.
6. Repeat the rhyme at the beginning of the next 3 to 5 lessons.
7. Using the Scrabble pieces, make words with vowel pairs such as *eat, sea, beat, boat, moan, rain, pail, feed,* and *teeth* and pronounce the words. The student may not be able to pronounce the entire word, but should be able to say the vowel pair. Praise

the student for saying the correct vowel pair, but tell him the correct pronunciation of the whole word also. If you have more than one student, have them prepare words for each other.

8. Have the student do the Vowel Pairs Worksheet in Appendix B9/CD.

Activity/Game

Bing-o for Vowel Pairs Game

- The teacher will need to play if there is only one student. Distribute the cards (from Appendix B10/CD).
- Shuffle the word cards, and then call out the long vowel words in random order. The students will find those words on their bingo cards. They will need to distinguish these from the words on their cards with short vowels.
- Students should cover the named word with a bingo chip. Bingo is called when a player covers a whole line.
- Check the card to make sure the words are correct.

Evaluation: Have the student read the following words:

1. Pail	5. Soap	8. Coat
2. Paint	6. Rain	9. Seat
3. Suit	7. Blue	10. Teen
4. Boat		

The student should be able to read 90 percent of the words. If he recognizes that the first vowel becomes long when followed by another vowel, he is considered correct—even if he does not get the rest of the word right. Give him the correct pronunciation afterward.

Hints for Accurate Reading

1. Ow and ou make a sound as if you were being pinched and said "Ow."

For example: *count, wow, out,* and *cow*

2. Oi and oy make the sound of a pig that says "oink."

For example: *oil, boil, boy, and toy*

3. *Oo* usually sounds like *"oooh."*

For example: *tooth, boo, fool, spook*

Lesson Three: C and G Sounds

The pronunciation of C and G usually depends on the letters (vowels) that follow them. C followed by E, I, and Y (when used as a vowel) is pronounced like /s/ in *cell*. When any other letters follow C, it is pronounced like /k/ as in *cat*. Similarly, G followed by E, I, and Y (when used as a vowel) is often pronounced like /j/ as in *gentle* or *giraffe*. Any other letters following G usually produce the sound of G as in *goat*, *got*, and *gag*. Sometimes these different pronunciations are called hard (followed by a, o, and u) and soft (followed by e, i, and y) sounds.

Objectives:

- The student will be able to correctly read words containing both pronunciations of C (hard and soft) depending on the vowels that follow.
- The student will be able to correctly read words containing both pronunciations of G (hard and soft) depending on the vowels that follow.

Materials:

- Small whiteboard or chalkboard
- Chalk or markers
- Worksheet on C (Appendix B11/CD)
- Worksheet on G (Appendix B12/CD)
- C and G Memory Game (Appendix B13/CD)

Success Step: Write the words cat and cell on the board. See if the student can read the words. Then read the words aloud, emphasizing the C sounds. Ask the student if the C in cat and the C in cell sound the same. (They don't.)

Procedure for Teaching about C:

- Have the student isolate the C sound in both C words and repeat both sounds.
- Work the following mini-worksheet with the student. Have the student underline the Cs in the words. Then have the student identify the vowel that comes after the C. If the vowel is /i/, /e/, or /y/, the C is soft and is pronounced like /s/. If the vowel is /o/, /u/, or /a/, the C is hard and is pronounced like /k/.
- Have the student do the Worksheet on C from Appendix B11/CD.

Mini-worksheet on C

Write the sound for /c/ after the written word—either /k/ or /s/. Put the letter between two slashes because the letter is used for a sound, not as part of a word.

cat __/k/__	cow _____	can _____	cage _____
cent _____	city _____	cell _____	copy _____

Visualization Hints

- Some students can learn which vowels are followed by hard or soft sounds by visualizing that the straight up and down vowels—I, E, and Y—are preceded by soft c, which is pronounced as /s/.
- The rounded vowels—O, U, and a—are proceeded by hard c, which is pronounced as /k/.

Procedure for Teaching about G:

- Write these words on the board: *Goat* and *Gem*. See if the student can read the words. Then read the words aloud, emphasizing the /G/ sounds. Ask the student if the G in *goat* and the G in *gem* sound the same.
- The G in *goat* is pronounced as /g/. The G in *gem* is pronounced as /j/.
- Have the student isolate the G sound in both G words and repeat both sounds.
- Work the following mini-worksheet with the student. Have the student underline the Gs in the words. Then have the student identify the vowel that comes after the G. If the vowel is /i/, /e/, or /y/, the G is often soft and is pronounced like /j/. If the vowel is /o/, /u/, or /a/, the G is usually hard and is pronounced like /G/.
- Have the student do the Worksheet on G from Appendix B12 or the CD.

Mini-worksheet on G

Write the sound for /g/ after the written word—either /j/ or /g/.

gym _____	gem _____	gap _____	got _____
go _____	guy _____	gin _____	giant _____

Activities/Games

Sorting Gs and Cs

- Cut out the C and G flashcards from the C and G Memory Game (Appendix B13/CD).
- Label half of an index card: Hard G /g/. Label another half of an index card: Soft G /j/. Place the cards in front of the students. Have the students take turns with the G flashcards sorting them under the labeled index cards.
- Label new half-index cards Hard C /k/ and Soft C /s/.
- Have the students take turns with the C flashcards sorting them under the labeled index cards
- When the students are successful with the individual sorting tasks, put all four half-index cards in front of the students and have them take turns sorting both the C and the G flashcards.

C and G Memory Game

- Using the same C and G flashcards that were used in the above sorting activity, place the cards in three rows of six each (printed side down).
- Have the student pick up and look at two cards. If the picture card matches the word card, the student should pronounce the word. If he pronounces it correctly, he gets to keep both cards. If there is no match, the student replaces both cards in the same place on the table.
- The next player then picks up two cards to try to find a match.
- Both players need to pay attention to where the cards are placed so they can make matches more easily.
- The player with the most matches at the end wins.
- The teacher sets the time limit on the game.

Example of C and G Word Flashcards

Generalization Activity

- Have the students look in their language experience stories (Part 2) and structured stories (Part 3) for words starting with /c/ and /g/. If there are not enough words in their stories, make up a few sentences with new words beginning with/c/ and /g/.

Evaluation: Have the student read the following words. He should be able to read 90 percent of them correctly. As long as he says the C and G sounds correctly, he can make mistakes on the rest of the word. The teacher should pronounce the word correctly each time.

1. Cone	6. Cell
2. Gas	7. Cent
3. George	8. Game
4. Gym	9. Gem
5. Cow	10. Cat

Lesson Four: Blends

Some phonics programs spend several lessons on consonant blends. In the Triangle Approach used in this book, we teach the general principle of blending consonants and expect the reader to apply that principle to many consonant blends. Most students learn blends by exposure to many words containing blends.

Objective: The student will be able to read consonant blends accurately.

Materials:

- Blends Worksheet from Appendix B14/CD
- Whiteboard or chalkboard
- Marker or chalk
- Cards from the Blends Memory Game (Appendix B15 or CD)

Success Step: Have the student tap out the letters of his name, one tap on the table for each letter in his name.

Procedure:

1. Tell the student that he has tapped out one tap for each letter in his name. If he needs more practice, have him tap out some more short words (without consonant blends).
2. Tell him that sometimes two or three consonants that are together need to be blended together so they only take one tap.
3. Have the student make the sound for /s/ and then the sound for /m/. Show him the word *small* written on the board. Tell him that /s/ and /m/ have to be blended together quickly so they only get one tap on the table. Have him say the combination /sm/ several times. Then have them say the word *small* several times. If he has

trouble with the concept, have him prolong the first sound with an "uh" behind it and then quickly say the rest of the word; e.g., suh-mall. Then have him say it faster so the consonants blend.

4. This lesson is intended to help the student learn the idea of blending a variety of consonants by practicing saying words. Have him practice the sounds of both consonants separately. Then have him say each word, blending the consonants.

5. Teachers and student(s) do the mini-worksheet on blends together. Have the student(s) circle the consonants that are together. Then have them say the word several times.

6. Have the student independently do the Blends Worksheet from Appendix B14 or CD.

Mini-worksheet on Blends

Spoon	Stamp
Block	Snake
Smile	Train
Cloud	Bread
Swing	Glove

Activity/Game

Blends Memory Game

- Cut out the blend flashcards (the text blends and the pictures) from Appendix B15 or print out from CD.
- Put the cards printed side down in three rows of six each.
- Have the student pick up and look at two cards. Have him read the word aloud. If the picture contains the written blend, the student keeps both cards. If there is no match, the student replaces both cards in the same place on the table.
- The next player looks at two cards. Since some of the pictures may suggest two words, those pictures have the beginning letter also in the square. Both the players need to pay attention to where the cards are placed so more matches can be made.
- The player with the most matches at the end wins.

Example: Blends Memory Game

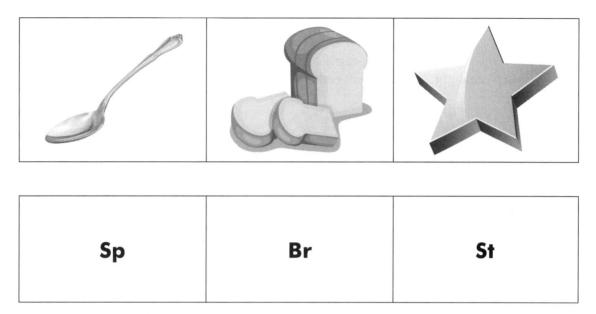

Sp	Br	St

Additional Hints for Accurate Reading

1. The K sound can often be written /ck/ in the middle or end of a word or syllable. It (ck) is counted as one sound. For example: *stick, thick,* and *quick.* You can tell the student: C and K kick together as /k/.

2. Sometimes the letter Y is used as a vowel as well as a consonant. When Y is at the beginning of a word or the beginning of a syllable, it is usually a consonant sound as in *yarn, yes,* or *yellow.* When Y ends a word or syllable or there is not another vowel in the syllable, Y usually takes the long sound of either /i/ or /e/.

   The students do not need to learn a rule here. They just need to know that Y at the beginning of a word is usually pronounced as *yuh.* Otherwise, the sound of Y (as a vowel) is either long /i/ or long /e/. The words *baby, family,* and *lady* are examples of a long /e/ sound. The words *cry, shy,* and *my* have the Y as a long /i/ sound. If the word has only one syllable, the /y/ is usually pronounced like long /i/ (*eye*). If the word has more than one syllable such as *worry,* the /y/ is usually pronounced like long /ee/.

   For practice with the Y sound, try the Starfall lesson on Y used as a vowel (below).

Starfall

- Go to the Starfall website on the Internet: www.starfall.com.
- Click on "Learn to Read."
- Go to Unit 15, under the "Play" heading. The first section is a Picture Hunt featuring Y as long /e/ sound. (The second section is a review of all vowels.)
- The book section is probably not age-appropriate for older students who are beyond the stage of using words like Mommy and Daddy.
- The skills video on Unit 15 is on Y as long /i/ or long /e/. Students could easily learn the long sounds that are presented here.

Word Endings

The most common word endings in English are /s/, /ed/, and /ing/. Many of the words the student is learning can have these common endings. First, the plural form of nouns will be taught. Then the verb endings of /ed/ and /ing/ will be taught with their meanings.

Lesson Five: Plurals

Objective: The student will be able to read plural nouns ending in /s/ and /es/.

Materials:

- A hat or bowl
- Paper squares of singular nouns (from Appendix or CD)
- Pencils
- Mini-worksheets 1 and 2, below
- M & Ms or other small candies, pretzels, etc.
- Tic Tac Toe Plural Game Sheets (B16 from Appendix/CD)

Success Step: Put up one arm. Say, "One arm. How would I say more than one arm?" Put both of your arms up. The student should say, "Two arms." If he says two or another number, he is correct. Note whether he adds the /s/ to the end of the word arm.

Procedures:

- Have the student put up one hand. Then say, "Put up two hands," emphasizing the final /s/.
- Hold up one pencil, saying "One pencil." Then put up two pencils, saying "Two _____ (with your voice going up in pitch), cueing the student to fill in the word *pencils*. If he does not add /s/, you model the word, emphasizing the /s/.
- Offer the student two M&Ms or other small food items and ask him what he wants. He should say, "Two candies" or "two M &Ms." Make sure he adds the /s/ to form the plural. If he does not, model the correct plural, emphasizing the /s/ sound. Then have him repeat it correctly and give him the M&Ms. Repeat until he gets the idea.
- Tell the students that when you want to talk about more than one thing, you usually just add /s/ to the end. Have the student fill in the following correct plurals orally:

Mini-worksheet 1 on Plurals

- One dog   Two __*dogs*__
- One book   Three _____
- One girl   Two _____
- One apple   Four _____
- One pear   Two _____
- One lake   Three _____
- One football Two _____

- Sometimes with words ending with a hissing sound (s, z, sh, ch), you need to add /es/. Write the word bus on a board or paper. Add another /s/ to the word—buss. Ask the student to try to pronounce that word. Ask him how you can tell that a word means more than one. Tell him that if you add /es/ to bus, it becomes *buses* and you can hear that it means more than one. Have the student fill in the following plurals correctly orally.

Mini-worksheet 2 on Plurals

- One box   Two _boxes_
- One peach   Three _____
- One brush   Four _____
- One glass   Two _____
- One watch   Four _____
- One dish   Two _____
- One kiss   Two _____
- One gas   Many _____

- Tell the student that some plurals are outlaws. They do not add /s/ or /es/. They actually change the word itself. The student will just have to memorize these words:
  - Child: Children
  - Man: Men
  - Mouse: Mice
  - Tooth: Teeth
  - Deer: Deer

- Write the plural of each of the nouns (name of a person, place, or thing) in the following sentence and make a new sentence:

A child, a man, and a mouse lost a tooth.

Activity/Game

Tic Tac Toe Plurals

- *Optional:* You and the student or two students can play the Tic Tac Toe Plurals game (Appendix B16/CD) for additional practice in adding /s/ or /es/ to form plurals.

Lesson Six: Past Tense Verbs Ending in /ed/

Objective: The student will be able to correctly read /ed/ endings for past tense.

Materials:

- Pencil
- Whiteboard or chalkboard and marker or chalk
- Past Tense Worksheet from Appendix B17 or CD

Success Step: Read the following sentences to the student. Ask him if the actions already happened or if they are happening right now.

Bill walked to the store. (Already happened)

Alex jumped down two steps. (Already happened)

If he answers correctly, ask the student how he knows. If he says the verbs *walked* or *jumped,* praise him and write the words on the board or paper, underlining the letters *ed.* If he is incorrect, model the correct pronunciation, emphasizing the *ed* and writing the words on the board or paper.

Procedures:

- Have the student tell you some action verbs such as *walk, jump, clap,* and *touch.* Make those verbs past tense by adding /ed/ to the verb. As you say /ed/, move your flat hand back over your shoulder (sign language for past tense). Your palm should face your body. Repeat with more action verbs, adding /ed/ and the hand movement for *past.*
- Most words already ending in /e/ such as *move, hope,* and *like* only add the /d/ to make past tense. If the words do not become past tense by adding /ed/ or /d/, tell the student that those words are *outlaws,* and they make the past tense in a different way. Examples include: go and went, come and came, take and took.
- If the student is in upper elementary or middle school, have him do the actions he has named. Ask him to indicate the past tense with the /ed/ ending by putting his arm and hand to the back of his shoulder as a sign for past tense, as done in some sign languages.
- Have the student do the Mini-worksheet on Past Tense below.
- Part of the worksheet consists of adding /ed/ to base words. The rest of the worksheet has the student remove the /ed/ from the words to disclose the base word:
- Have the student do the Past Tense Worksheet from Appendix B17 or CD.

Mini-worksheet on Past Tense

Add /d/ or /ed/	Remove /d/ or /ed/
- watch — watched	jumped
- pick —	walked
- work —	shined

Note: At this point we don't worry about the spelling rules for past tense. However, the student may encounter some words that end in a consonant and /y/ in which the /y/ changes to /i/ before adding /ed/. For example, *cry* becomes *cried, fry* become *fried,* and *bury* becomes *buried.* The student should be able to recognize the /ied/ as a past tense ending of the verb.

Lesson Seven: Present Tense Continuous Action Verbs Ending in /ing/

Objective: The student will be able to correctly read /ing/ endings for ongoing actions.

Materials:

- Continuous Actions Worksheet (Appendix B18/CD)
- Pencil
- Whiteboard or chalkboard and marker or chalk

Success Step: Have the student put the action words jump, skip, and look into past tense by adding /ed/.

Procedures:

- Tell the student that sometimes an action word needs to show that the action is ongoing at the time. Usually it begins with a form of a *to be* verb such as *is, am, are.* Then the base word adds an */ing/* ending. Read the following sentences to the student and ask if the action is going on.

I am walking outside.

He is talking very loudly.

- Write some action words (verbs) on the board or paper.
- Ask the student to make these words show that the action is ongoing:

I am play____ outside.

David is paint____ the room.

Joleen is take____ the books down.

The man is cook____ the dinner.

- Have the student name some more action verbs. You add a *to be* word and then have the student add */ing/* to the action word.
- Some of the words your student gives may end in silent *e.* Just as when adding *ed,* you drop the /e/ when adding *ing.* If the student does not give you a word ending in silent *e,* put the word *make* on the board or paper and ask how you should add *ing.* Put the word *making* on the board. Have the student add *ing* to the words:

Make	**Cook**
Bite	**Talk**
Race	**Look**
Bake	**Say**

- Have the student do the Continuous Actions Worksheet from Appendix B18 or CD.
- Remind the student that with words such as *hike* and *race* ending in silent e, you drop the *e* and add */ing/*
- There are some short-vowel words ending in a consonant in which the consonant is doubled before adding ed or ing, but we are not introducing that at this time.

Activity/Game

Tic Tac Toe Word Endings Game

- Make several Tic Tac Toe boards with /ed/, /d/, or /ing/ endings in different squares (from Appendix B19 or CD).
- Cut out the squares containing the appropriate phrases (with the root word) from the Appendix and put them in a hat or a bowl.
- The first student pulls a square out of the hat or bowl and reads the phrase with the root word. The teacher may help him read the phrase or the word.
- The student says the appropriate form of the word and puts the phrase square on the game sheet on either /ing/, /ed/, or /d/. If he is incorrect, he puts the phrase square back into the hat/bowl
- The next student or the teacher pulls another square out and reads it. Then he says the appropriate form of the root word and continues.
- The first one to fill his card wins. You can shorten the game by requiring a smaller number of squares to win. You can exchange game boards for a second round.
- See if the student can figure out that when there is a form of the verb *to be* (is, am, are, etc.), the action word following will take an *ing* ending. Otherwise, the word will take an /ed/ or /d/ ending. Remind him that if the word ends with a silent /e/, you just add /d/.

Note: There is not a Starfall program that explains word endings.

Generalization Activity

- Look back at the Learning Experience and Structured Stories the student has been reading. Have him find some /ed/ and /ing/ words.

Evaluation: Have the student write the word in parentheses with the correct ending. For example: Last week Amy (jump) <u>jumped</u> over the fence.

1. Eddie is (sit) _____ on the chair.

2. I am (walk)_____ .

3. Yesterday Dan (work)_____ for 8 hours.

4. Fern (wash) _____ the dog last night.

5. Two (bug) _____ crawled in the room.

6. Four (dress) _____ were too long.

7. Three (man) _____ went to my house.

8. Two (wheel) _____ were missing.

9. I (burn) _____ my finger.

10. Four (child) _____ came late.

The student should be able to complete 90 percent of the sentences correctly. If he writes the endings correctly, he is considered correct.

Level Three Phonics

By the time students reach Level 3, they should be able to sound out most one-syllable words, with the exception of words with r-controlled vowels. They'll learn how to do that in this level. Most simple phonics books end their instruction at this point. However, many older struggling students are not able to transfer what they have learned about reading one-syllable words to multi-syllable words. Therefore, Level 3 in the Triangle Approach includes an introduction to syllabication and multisyllabic words, including prefixes, suffixes, and contractions. By the end of this level, students should be able to read some high-low books written on a second- to third-grade level. These multiple syllable concepts are quite difficult, however. If your students do not master all these concepts (syllabication, etc.), revisit them as you make the transition to general reading books.

Lesson One: R-Controlled Vowels

When the letter *r* follows a vowel, it changes the sound of that vowel somewhat. Linguists have found it difficult to write a clear r-controlled phonics rule because dialects of English vary according to the speaker's location and culture (Trammell, 1982).

Most of the vowels followed by *r* are pronounced */er/*. This means that the r-controlled vowels in *dollar, bird, turkey, summer, shirt,* and *color* are decoded as *er* (sometimes shown as schwa r). There are times, however, when */or/* or */ar/* are pronounced with more of the sound of the original vowel, such as in the words *cork, fork, corn, car, far, park,* and *card.* Again, you may want to remind the student that words that do not follow the rules are called **outlaws.** (The outlaw concept is used for other words that do not follow phonics rules, not just r-controlled words.)

Objective: The student will be able to recognize r-controlled vowels and decode them as *er* or as *or* (*for*) or *ar* (car).

Materials:

- R-Controlled Crossword Puzzles #1 and #2 (Appendix B20 and B21)
- Pencil
- Whiteboard or paper, marker

Success Step: Have the student(s) tell you all the vowels.

Procedure:

- Tell the students that when a vowel is followed by the letter r, it changes the sound of the vowel. Write some words using r-controlled vowels on paper or a whiteboard: *bird, hurt, water,* and *hammer.*
- Ask the students to point out the vowels with r following them in the above words.
- Tell the students that most of the time the vowel-plus-r combination is pronounced /er/ (or schwa r). Have the students pronounce the /er/ sound several times.
- Look at each of the sample words:

  B **ir** d = er

  H **ur** t = er

  Wat **er** = er

  Hamm **er** = er

- Discuss more r-controlled words: *fur, girl, paper, church, shirt, turkey, flower, skirt, clerk, her, worry,* and *turn.*
- Tell the students that sometimes the combinations /or/ and /ar/ are not pronounced /er/ but sound more like the letters o or a and then r. Examples of these outlaws are *horse, farm, far, fork, cart,* and *star.* To help them get the contrast between the /er/ and /or/ or /ar/, have them pronounce the /or/ and /ar/ words as if they were /er/ words. *Farm* would then sound like *firm, far* would sound like *fur, star* like *stir,* and *cart* like *curt.*
- Tell the students that they should try the /er/ sound first and if it doesn't sound like a word (or sounds like another word that does not make sense in the sentence), try the sounds of /or/ or /ar/.

 **Activity/Game**

Crossword Puzzles

- Give the students the R-controlled Crossword Puzzle #1 from the Appendix or CD.
- Explain the across and down questions and how to put the letters in the proper boxes. Show your student(s) the words to choose from at the bottom of the puzzle.
- Do the first two words together. Then have the students do the puzzle independently.
- Correct the puzzle with the students.
- Do the R-Controlled Vowel Crossword Puzzle #2 next. If you want to make a competition out of the puzzles, have the first person to finish with all correct answers be the winner.

Starfall

- Log on to the Starfall website at www.starfall.com.
- Click on "Learn to Read," Unit 13, Play section.
- The Play section supplies words that match pictures, giving the student practice on words with /or/. As the student is able to read the /or/ words, the pictures become colored in.
- The Book section in Unit 13 has a story that uses words that contain /or/.
- Continue on to Unit 14 for exercises on schwa r, which is described as /ir/.
- The Play section in Unit 14 has a word-sort activity featuring /ar/, /or/, and /ir/.
- Unit 14 covers r-controlled vowels /er/, /ir/, and /ur/ that are pronounced like /er/ in a Play section called "Make a Match." The second part of the Play section has a word-sort activity featuring /ar/, /or/, and /ir/. However, since Starfall has not explained the r-controlled sound of /ar/, you may have to explain that sound before your student(s) can sort the words. You may also need to remind your students that /ir/ has the same sound as /er/.
- The Book section of Unit 14 also has many r-controlled words.

Generalization Activity

- Have the student find r-controlled vowels in her Language Experience stories or in the Structured Stories in Part 3 of this book. If these stories do not have enough r-controlled vowels, write several sentences with unfamiliar words having r-controlled words in them: "It is dark in the yard, but I see Bert burning leaves next to the church."

Evaluation: Have the student read the following words:

1. Her	5. Horse	8. Farm
2. Fork	6. Dirt	9. Sister
3. Turn	7. Burn	10. Girl
4. Pork		

She should get 90 percent of them correct. If not, spend more time on r-controlled vowels in Starfall.

Dividing Multisyllabic Words into Syllables

In Levels One and Two, students learned how to decode mostly short, one-syllable words. These skills need to be extended to longer words, mainly by teaching the students to divide the words into syllables. Some students just give up when they see longer words.

Lesson Two: Putting Syllables Together

Objective: The student will be able to make actual compound words out of short words.

Materials:

- Index cards, Compound Words Game (from Appendix B22 or CD), and glue
- *OR* Compound Words (from Appendix B22 or CD), copied onto cardstock
- Scissors

Success Step: One way to teach about syllables is to have the student make words herself by combining two words (syllables) to make compound words. Ask the student if she can make one word out of the two words hair and cut. She should say, "Haircut." Ask her to form other compound words such as pan cake, milk shake, bath robe, cow boy, etc.

Procedures:

- Tell the student that those words are called compound words—words that are made of two complete other words.
- Then play the *Match Game* with her.

 Activity/Game

Match Game

- Cut twelve index cards in half.
- Using the short words from Appendix B22 or CD, glue the initial words close to the right side of the card and the second part of the word close to the left side of the card. Thus, it will be easy to put the cards together to look like a compound word.
- *OR* copy the small words from the Appendix or CD from onto cardstock and cut out the cards.

back	yard

- Have the students make compound words with the cards. At first the teacher should hand out only four compound words at a time. The students should be able to match up the 4 initial words with the 4 secondary words to make 4 real compound words. Later, hand out 8 or 12 initial and secondary words and make the task more difficult.

Initial	**Second**
apple	sauce
air	plane

- On lined paper, have the students write the new compound words they have made with the flashcards.

Lesson Three: Breaking Compound Words into Syllables

Now the students are going to do the reverse of the above (making compound words out of two small words). Present the following compound words to the student and have them separate out the small words—thus isolating the syllables, e.g., barefoot—bare/foot (2 syllables), baseball—base/ball (2 syllables), desktop—desk/top (2 syllables).

Objective: The student will be able to separate compound words into their syllables.

Materials:

- Large mirror or small mirrors that each student can see
- List of one- to three-syllable words from student's stories or the words from Appendix B22

Success Step: Have the student tell you three compound words.

Procedure:

- Do the following mini-worksheet with the student.

Mini-worksheet on Separating Compound Words into Syllables

popcorn	pop/corn	2 syllables
classroom	class/room	2 syllables
homework		
cupcake		
pancake		
backyard		

- Have the student tap out each part of the previous mini-sheet compound words with her finger or a pencil eraser on the table. Tell her that she is tapping out the *syllables* of the words.
- Tell her that other noncompound, longer words can also be broken into syllables.
- Have the student look in the mirror while she says the following words: art, bulldog, reading, butterfly.
- Tell the student that each time her mouth drops, it means one syllable. Tell her that each syllable has to have one vowel. When you say a vowel, it makes your mouth open and your jaw drops.

Lesson Four: Counting Syllables

Objective: The student will be able to count syllables in noncompound words.

Materials:

- Whiteboard and marker
- Worksheet on Dividing Words into Syllables (Appendix B23)

To really become proficient at decoding unfamiliar multisyllabic words, students need to be able to divide the long words into syllables. Once a word is divided into shorter syllables, the student can use the phonics she has previously learned to decode the word

Success Step: Review which letters are vowels. Have the student repeat (by memory) the small chart at the end of the following list of vowels (A—apple—a).

Vowel Review

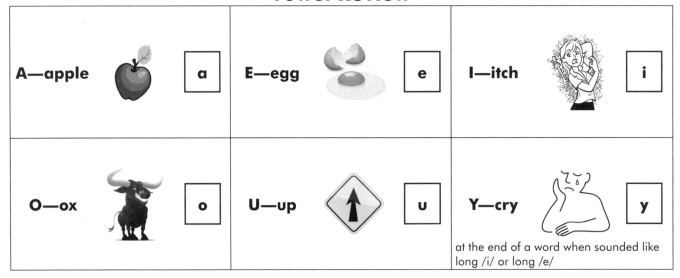

| A—apple | a | E—egg | e | I—itch | i |
| O—ox | o | U—up | u | Y—cry | y |

at the end of a word when sounded like long /i/ or long /e/

Procedure:

- Show the student two words with one and two syllables written on the whiteboard or chalkboard. Say the words, tapping the syllables. Write more one-, two-, and three-syllables words on the board. Have the student read the words, tapping out the syllables and telling the count. You can help her with reading the words. If she has trouble, have her look in the mirror and watch her jaw. She may also put her hand underneath her jaw to feel the jaw movements.

- Tell the student that each syllable must have one vowel in it. That is an important clue for figuring out syllables.
- Point out the vowels in the following mini-worksheet. Underline each vowel. Count two vowels together (which have one long sound) as one vowel. Don't count silent /e/ as a vowel. Count digraphs (H words like /ph/, /wh/, th/, /sh/, and /ch/ as one sound. This total number should tell you how many syllables are in the word).

Mini-worksheet on Counting Syllables

Teacher and student do the mini-worksheet together. Underline the vowel(s). When there are 2 vowels that sound as one vowel, it counts as one vowel. Count digraphs (H words like /ph/, /wh/, th/, /sh/, and /ch/ as one sound. Count the number of syllables.

better	___	**write**	___	**water**	___
boss	___	**baby**	___	**open**	___
zebra	___	**yellow**	___	**apple**	___
horse	___	**hippo**	___	**sweater**	___
order	___	**dinner**	___	**zipper**	___
wolf	___	**panda**	___	**mitten**	___

- Have the student do the Worksheet on Dividing Words into Syllables (Appendix B23).

The student should now be able to count the number of syllables in the word either by counting the vowels or by feeling her jaw drop when she pronounces a syllable. She should be able to tell the various syllables of a word, even if she has not learned the rules of syllabication. For example, the word *summer* has two vowels—/u/and /e/—and has two syllables. If you say the word *summer*, you can feel your jaw drop two times—*sum/mer*. The student *should* be able to pronounce the small word *sum* and the small word *mer* using the knowledge she has already learned.

Syllabification is not an easy task for students. You don't have to teach everything about it to the student(s), even in Level 4. The most important use for it is in decoding unfamiliar words. If the student can divide longer words into smaller syllables, then she will be able to decode much longer, more difficult words.

Note: Some older students may need more detail on how exactly the words are divided. Some students may need to learn at least some of the syllabification rules so they know where to divide the words into syllables. For example, the rule that a word is divided into syllables between two middle consonants can be used to separate words like plan/ning rab/bit, lit/tle, and pur/ple. Some students may need to see the parts of a word written with a slash to know how to decode the word. A section on how exactly to divide words into syllables is provided as an optional Level 4 in Chapter 9.

Lesson Five: Prefixes and Suffixes

In Level Two, students learned about the verb ending of /ing/, as well as the past tense adding /d/ or /ed/. They also learned about the plural ending /es/ or /s/ added to nouns that end in a hissing sound.

In Level Three, students are ready to learn about other suffixes added to the ends of root words, as well as prefixes added to the beginnings of words. Learning the meanings of common prefixes and suffixes can expand a student's reading vocabulary. Prefixes and suffixes are separate syllables added to the base word.

Objectives:

- The student will be able to identify common prefixes in multisyllabic words.
- The student will be able to identify common suffixes in multisyllabic words.

Materials:

- Prefixes Worksheet (Appendix B24 or CD)
- Suffixes Worksheet (Appendix B25 or CD)
- Whiteboard or chalkboard
- Marker or chalk
- Copy of common prefixes in text, Appendix, or CD for each student
- Copy of common suffixes in text, Appendix, or CD for each student
- Copy of Prefixes and Suffixes Crossword Puzzle (Appendix B26) for each student

Success Step: Have the student repeat the words prefix and suffix after you. Explain what the two words mean to the student. Have the student say the words a second time.

Prefixes

Procedure: Show the student the list of common prefixes below:

Prefix	Meaning	Example	Prefix	Meaning	Example
Un	not	untie	**Dis**	not	disable
Pre	before	prepay	**In, Im**	not	imperfect
Re	again	replay	**Sub**	under	subway
Non	not	nonsense	**Anti**	against	antifreeze
Il, ir	not	illegal	**De**	opposite	defrost
Mis	not	misspell	**Bi**	two	bifocals

- The student does not have to memorize the prefixes or their meanings. She should, however, be able recognize prefixes and realize that they usually add a syllable to the root word and change the meaning.
- Do the mini-worksheet with the student on paper or on the whiteboard or chalkboard.
- Discuss the meanings of the words on the mini-worksheet.

Mini-worksheet on Prefixes

No. of Syllables	Division	No. of Syllables	Division
____ Return	re turn	____ Mistrust	
____ Subway		____ Preview	
____ Misfire		____ Undone	
____ Rerun		____ Detour	

■ Have the student do the Prefix Worksheet from the Appendix and correct it with her orally, if possible. Talk about the meanings of the words.

Generalization Activities
■ Look at the Language Experience stories the student has written. Have her find the words that have prefixes. Have her read the words.
■ If the student's stories do not include appropriate words, make up some sentences with prefixes. She does not need to be able to read the rest of the sentence. For example: I want to redo my cake but not from underneath the table.
■ Point out prefixes as the student reads new stories.

Suffixes

Procedure: Show the student the list of common suffixes.

Suffix	Meaning	Example	Suffix	Meaning	Example
Er	worker of (or comparative)	farmer	tion, sion (pronounced shun)	act of	action
Est	most	smallest	less	without	fearless
Ful	full of	careful	ing	act of	going
Able/Ible	can be done	breakable	ly	characteristic of	quickly
Ment	act of	government	ful	full of	tearful
Ness	state of	kindness	al/ial	having characteristic of	personal

■ The student does not have to memorize the suffixes or their meanings. She should, however, be able recognize suffixes and realize that they usually add a syllable to the root word.
■ Do the mini-worksheet with the student on paper or on the whiteboard or chalkboard.

Mini-worksheet on Suffixes

Word	Underline suffix	Word	Underline suffix
careful	care <u>ful</u>	worker	
walked		helpless	
imagination		biggest	
helpfully		tallest	

- Have the student do the Suffix Worksheet (from Appendix B25) independently and correct it with her orally, if possible. Discuss the meanings of the words.

 **Activities/Games**

Crossword Puzzle

- Do the *Prefixes and Suffixes Crossword Puzzle* from Appendix B26 or CD.

Generalization Activities

- Look at the Language Experience stories the student has written and the Structured Stories in Part 3. Have the student find the words that have suffixes. Have her read the words.
- If the student's stories do not include appropriate words, make up some sentences with suffixes. She does not need to be able to read the rest of the sentence. For example: The endless noise didn't sound wonderful to the pianist.
- Point out suffixes as the student reads new stories.

Evaluation: Circle the prefix or suffix in each word.

1. Rewrite
2. Unhappy
3. Smaller
4. Preview
5. Speechless
6. Largest
7. Subway
8. Baker
9. Helpful
10. Untie

The student does not have to separate the syllables in the words. She just needs to recognize the prefixes and suffixes and circle them. If she does not get 80 percent correct, give her additional practice in recognizing prefixes and suffixes.

Lesson Six: Contractions

By now, the student should have written many language experience stories with you and has probably used contractions in at least several of her stories. She should be able to read these contractions, since she knows what happens in her own stories. Now, however, you want to ensure that she can read and understand all contractions commonly used in English.

Contractions are shortened versions of the written and spoken forms of a word. They result from combining two words and leaving out certain letters to make the word shorter. The letters that are left out are replaced by an apostrophe. For example, the /o/ in *not* is left out in *doesn't* and the /a/ in *am* is left out in *I'm*.

The following are the most common contractions. The words below the contractions are some of the words that can take that contraction.

'll (will)	**'s** (is or has)	**'d** (had or would)	**'re** (are)
he, I, she, they	he, she, it	He, she, they, we, you, I	you, they, we
you, we, it	let, there		

n't (not)	**'ve** (have)	**'m** (am)	
are, can, could, does, do, had, has, have, might, must, should,	I, you, they, we	I	

Objective: The student will be able to identify what common contractions stand for.

Materials:

- Match Game of Contractions from Appendix B27/CD
- Whiteboard or chalkboard
- Marker or chalk

Success Step: Ask the student to repeat some of the above contractions after you say them.

Procedure:

- Ask the student(s) if they know a shorter way to say: "Do not touch!" Tell them how to do it if they can't come up with "Don't touch!" Write "Do not = don't" on the board. Can they tell you a shorter way to say: "We are number one"? "I am first"? "You can not catch me"? etc. Write "We are = we're," etc. on the board.
- Tell the students that this way of combining two words into one is called a contraction.
- Have them look at the equivalents you've written down (do not = don't) and see if they can tell you what letter was removed.

- Cross that letter out and show how an apostrophe is substituted in the word.
- Have the students practice making their own contractions. For example, tell them, "If you add an 'apostrophe ll' to a word, it means *will*. So, what is another way to say "they will"? See if the students can name other contractions.
- Work the mini-worksheet with the student telling what the contractions stand for.

Mini-worksheet on Contractions

Contraction	Stands for	Contraction	Stands for
can't	can not	won't	
I'm		I'll	
didn't		you'll	
what's		they're	
isn't		she's	

Activities/Games

Contraction Match

- Cut out the contractions and the meaning cards from Appendix B27. If you have several students, you may need to run the cards off on cardstock paper.
- Put the cards face down, 4 rows of 5. The student turns over any two cards. If the contraction matches the meaning card, the student takes the two cards and continues playing. If they do not match, the student puts them down in the same places they came from, and the next person takes her turn.
- Continue playing until all the cards are matched.

Example:

They'll	They will	You're	You are
We've	We have	I'm	I am
We'd	We would	She's	She is

Generalization Activities

- Go to the Language Experience stories the student has written. Have the student find contractions.
- If the student's stories do not include any contractions, go to the Structured

Stories in Part 3 and have her point out contractions. She does not have to read all the sentences, just point out the contractions.

■ Look at ads/headlines in the newspaper or magazines and find the contractions. Say what they mean.

Evaluation: Have the student tell what the following contractions mean. She should get 90 percent correct.

1. They'll	5. I'm	8. Doesn't
2. We'd	6. He's	9. I've
3. Wasn't	7. You'll	10. Can't
4. Don't		

Optional
Level Four Phonics:
Syllable Division Rules

In Level Three Phonics, the student learned how to count and distinguish syllables. He learned to count syllables by counting the number of vowels in the word and by lowering his jaw each time a new syllable starts. If the student needs to learn how to divide words into syllables more precisely, he can learn the rules below and apply them to the words he reads.

Lesson One: Syllable Rules

Success Step: Review which letters are vowels.

Materials:

- Copy of Syllable Rules from Appendix B29
- Mini-worksheet on Dividing Words into Syllables (not including Opened/Closed Syllables)
- Mini-worksheet on Open/Closed Syllables from the text
- Worksheet on Dividing CVC Words into syllables from Appendix B28/CD
- Copy of graphics on Open & Closed Syllables from text or Appendix B30/CD

Procedure:

- Review the rules about syllables that the student already knows:
  - ➤ **Every syllable has one vowel sound.** Write the students' names on the board. Teacher and students underline the vowels in the names. (At first put a small /v/ under each vowel.) Count the vowels in the words to tell you how many syllables in the word. (If a name includes two adjacent vowels that make one sound, remind the student of the rule "when two vowels go walking, the second one usually does the talking.")
    Note: /Y/ can be a vowel if it has the sound of long /e/ or /i/.

> ➤ **A compound word is divided between the small words that make up the compound word;** e.g., cup / cake, base / ball, tooth / brush
> ➤ **A prefix or suffix is a separate syllable;** e.g., <u>re</u>/main, <u>un</u>/tie, <u>sub</u>/way or care/<u>less</u>, farm/<u>er</u>, and na /<u>tion.</u>

- Introduce these additional rules:
  - ➤ Separate 2 consonants (including double consonants) in the middle of the word; e.g., win/ter, fas/ter, gar/den, but/ter.
    Note: Do not separate consonant digraphs that have one sound (ch, sh, th, ph, wh) or blends such as bl, sk, cl, dr, and fl.
  - ➤ A consonant in front of *le* makes a syllable; e.g., ta/ble, cir/cle, bat/tle, pur/ple. (The /le/ is pronounced /el/.)
  - ➤ When a vowel is sounded alone in a word, it forms a syllable by itself; e.g., <u>u</u> / nit, <u>a</u>/pril, and ed/<u>u</u>/cation

- Teacher and student discuss the mini-worksheet on dividing words into syllables. For each word, give the reason for the division.

Mini-worksheet Dividing Words in Syllables

Word	Reason	Word	Reason
little (lit/tle) together (to/gether)	2 consonants compound word	dinner (din/ner) summer (sum/mer)	2 consonants 2 consonants
true football		wishful number	
game rabbit		mother safety	
wonderful city		ladder great	

- Have the student independently do the Worksheet on Dividing Words into Syllables from Appendix B23 (this is a repeat of the worksheet done in Chapter 8).
- Correct the worksheet orally with the student.

Open and Closed Syllables in CVC Words

The most difficult division of words occurs when there is a consonant, vowel, consonant (CVC) in the middle of a word. You have to decide whether the word divides after the first vowel or after the consonant. This makes a difference in reading because the first vowel is pronounced either long or short depending on where the word is divided. For example, the word *cabin* can be divided cab / in or ca / bin. If the first syllable is /cab/, the /a/ is short and the last syllable is /in/. It will be called a closed syllable. If the first syllable is /ca/, the /a/ is long and the last syllable is /bin/. It will be called an open syllable. If you do not know the word, you just have to pronounce it both ways and see which makes sense as a word. Is it pronounced /kab/in/ or kay/bin/?

Older students should be able to recognize commonly used words.

- Use the graphics below (and in Appendix B30) to help the student learn the two options for a CVC (consonant/vowel/consonant) combination in the middle of a word.

1. Divide after the consonant—e.g., cab/in. In dividing after the consonant, the syllable *cab* has a **short** vowel /a/ in it. This syllable is called closed—CVC.

Closed Syllable

The vowel (girl) is <u>closed</u> in by a consonant (boy) on both sides. She can't run.
*The vowel is **short**.*

2. Divide after the vowel—e.g., ba/sic. In dividing after the vowel, the syllable *ba* has a **long** vowel /a/ ending it. It is called open syllable (CV, V)

Open Syllable

The vowel (girl) can run away because the consonant (boy) is only on one side.
*The syllable is **open**. The vowel is long (says its own name).*

- The student needs to try to divide the syllable both ways. Determine which way makes a recognizable word.

■ The National Education Support Service describes these two options as the **Spider Rule** and the **Camel Rule** (www.educsupport.com).

The Spider Rule and the Camel Rule

Spi der rule—divide after the vowel, making the vowel long (saying its alphabet name)

Cam el rule—divide after the consonant, making the vowel short.

■ The Open/Closed Syllable Rule can make quite a difference in a student's ability to decode multisyllabic words. Usually older students have enough of a listening vocabulary that they can recognize which pronunciation makes a real word. For example, the word *shiver* could be divided after the vowel—*shi/ver*. The vowel /i/ would then be long and the word would be pronounced shi*(eye)/* ver. That's not a familiar word. If shiver is divided after the consonant /v /, it becomes the familiar word *shiver*. The student has to make a choice based on his receptive knowledge of the language. However, you should certainly discuss meanings of all the words decoded.

■ Do the Mini-worksheet on CVC Open/Closed Syllables together with the student, explaining your reasons for the choice.

Mini-worksheet on CVC Open/Closed Syllables

Word	Reason	Word	Reason
Hotel	closed—hot/el open—ho/tel	Baby	closed—bab/y open—ba/by
Robot		Cub	
Comet		Fabric	

■ Have the student independently do the Worksheet on Dividing CVC Words into Syllables.

Activity/Game

Generalization Activities

- Look at the Language Experience stories the student has written. Have him find the words that have two or more syllables and then read the words. See if separating the multisyllabic words helps him to decode the longer words.
- If the student's stories do not include appropriate words, make up some sentences with two or more syllables. For example: In the education library, he drew a little circle in the middle of the paper that listed the books he needed.
- When the student stumbles when reading multisyllabic words, stop him and remind him to think about the rules for syllabification. If necessary, point out that there are two consonants in a row, etc., to remind him of the rule.

Evaluation: Divide the following words into syllables:

Yellow	Marble
Dinner	Happy
Able	Evil
Windmill	Kidnap
Dentist	Wedding

The student should be able to divide 90 percent of the words correctly.

For Further Work on Syllabification

If you wanted to teach a language arts lesson in syllabification, you would need to do many more examples with your student(s). In this optional chapter, I have only introduced the rules of syllabification that relate to decoding multisyllabic words. If you want to pursue more work on multi-syllable words, I suggest the books in the *Rewards* series by Anita Archer, Mary Gleason, and Vicky Vachon, published by Sopris West.

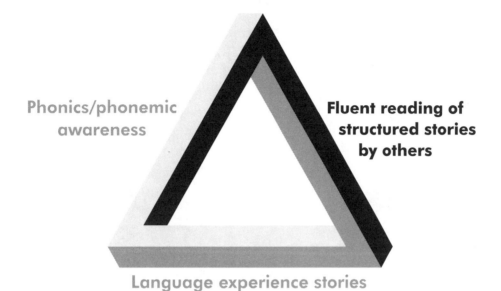

Phonics/phonemic awareness

Fluent reading of structured stories by others

Language experience stories (Base)

Chapter 10: Structured Stories (by other authors)

- Level One
    - One Way
    - Cookies
    - Shadows
    - Bill
    - Hunting
    - Trouble
    - What I Hear
    - Hot
    - Rain Plus
    - Swim
    - The Sandwich #1

- Level Two
    - The Sandwich #2
    - Daniel
    - How We Got the Ohio River
    - Summer Camp
    - Brownies
    - The Big Snow Storm
    - Shark
    - Coming Through

- Level Three
    - My Alien Friend
    - Hidden
    - Magic Under Ice
    - Speed Demon
    - My Skateboard
    - Fishing
    - Glass

10

Structured Stories

An important part of the Triangle Approach is to have students repeatedly read stories—both the language experience stories they write themselves in Part 1 and the structured stories written by other authors that are included in this section. This step is aimed at increased fluency, an important factor in the National Reading Panel's list of reading principles. Students read and reread a text a certain number of times or until a certain level of fluency is reached. For most struggling older readers, you should plan on four re-readings at a minimum for most stories. The student(s) should read the story with expression in phrases and with no more than one mistake.

Reading fluency can be developed gradually over time and through practice. You, the teacher, can also help your students develop fluency by modeling fluent reading.

The stories in this section have been structured to gradually expose the students to higher-level reading skills as they progress through the levels. These structured stories have been leveled with the Flesch-Kincaid Grade Level Readability Formula, which takes into account the average sentence length and number of syllables per word. In addition, I have applied more descriptive measures such as complexity of the story, pictures telling part of story, repetition of words and phrases, predictability of content, and size and layout of print (Rog & Burton, 2001; Fountas & Pinnell, 1999; Hiebert, 1999).

In reading structured stories with your student(s), you should use teaching techniques that are similar to those you use with the students' language experience stories. However, you will need to introduce each new structured story to your students more systematically.

Here is the recommended procedure for using structured stories in the Triangle Approach to teaching reading:

- Talk about the title of the story with the student.
- Look at the illustrations in the story and discuss them with the student.

- Introduce the new vocabulary words by looking at them in the story and having the student pronounce them.
- Have the "football" word cards (Appendix A2) ready for the new story.
- Read the story to the student.
- Then read the story together with the student.
- Have the student read the story independently, supplying any words that she doesn't know.
- Read the story together, varying approaches such as alternating words or sentences or having another student read some of the conversations.
- Put the "footballs" out in front of the student.
- Have the student read the words he or she knows in isolation. Make a pile of incorrect words and a pile of correct words.
- Locate the missed words in the story and compare the "football" word to its use in the story.
- Have the student read the story at subsequent sessions until she can read it with 100 percent accuracy or with only one word missed.

STARTER STORY: One Way

Vocabulary (for Pre-Teaching)

Sight Words	Content Words
one	way crash

The first story is a starter story to engage the student in an action that is easy to predict and will help her experience success in reading. If the student is young, use two Matchbox or other toy cars and do the actions in the story. If not, show the first two pictures to the student and ask what is going to happen.

One Way

CRASH

Cookies?

Vocabulary

Sight Words	Content Words
is	Mexico
in	food
are	dog
she	Fran
good	buys
they	cookies
for	
no	

This story has eight sight words that are very commonly used. Be sure to preteach the names *Fran* and *Mexico*. Mexico is a longer word, but you can talk about the students' experiences with travel and friends from Mexico and capture their interest. The content words have many uses of /o/, /oo/, and /ou/.

Consider giving the students cookies or bringing in sample packages of cookies and dog food. Ask the students how Fran must have felt when she found out she bought dog food instead of cookies. Why do they think Fran did not read the words *dog food* on the package? See if they can infer that the package is in Spanish.

Cookies?

Fran is in Mexico.

She buys cookies.

"Good cookies!"

"No, they are for dog food!"

Level One   **Structured Stories**

Shadows

Vocabulary

Sight Words	Content Words
I	shadows
see	woman
of	wall
a	boy
my	girl
on	surprise
the	family
	more

Already learned: they, in, is, she

This story may be longer than previous stories, but many of the words are repeated: "I see _____"; "of a _____ on the wall." The pattern makes the reading easier. The words *woman, man, boy,* and *girl* may also be familiar to the student from incidental learning.

Introduce the words first, using the pictures in the story. Be sure to pre-teach the words *shadow* and *surprise.* This is a good story for choral reading with several students.

Shadows

I see shadows.

I see the shadow of a man on the wall.

I see the shadow of a woman on the wall.

I see the shadow of a boy on the wall.

I see the shadow of a girl on the wall.

I see more shadows on the wall.

Surprise! They are shadows of my family.

Bill

Vocabulary

Sight Words	Content Words
walks	store
buys	candy bar
says	lost
gets	thank
you	takes
	home
	cop (policeman)

Already learned: the, a, to,

Beginning with this story, there will be content questions on each story. You do not need to test the student's comprehension until she can read the story fluently. She should not have to worry about decoding the words while she is thinking about the meaning of the content. You may read the questions to the student at first. Later you may want to have her read the questions, if you know that she understands all the words in the question.

Content Questions
1. Bill bought _____ from the store.
2. _____ helped Bill when he was lost.
3. Bill said "_____" to the cop (policeman) when he got home.
4. Bill _____ed to the store.
5. Did Bill have any money? How do you know?

Bill

Bill walks.

Bill walks to the store.

Bill buys a candy bar.

Bill gets lost.

Bill runs to a cop.

The cop takes Bill home.

"Thank you," says Bill.

Level One   *Structured Stories*

Hunting

This story is one of the examples of language experience stories given in Part 1. For the student, it will be a structured story by another author, but it will have the same feel as a language experience story.

Vocabulary

Sight Words	Content Words
we	feet
my	wet
don't	deer
go	face
	rain(s)
	hard
	Dad
	hunt(ing)

Already learned: I

Pictures carry most of the story. The sentences are short and directly relate to the pictures. The story is not really pleasant, but it is real. The grammar is not corrected. You may change the last sentence from "We don't get no deer" to "We didn't get any deer" if you are concerned about giving a correct grammar model. However, the students do relate to this language, and you can ask them how to say the sentence correctly.

Content Questions
1. True or False: The writer went hunting all by himself.
2-3. The writer got his _____ and his _____ wet.
4. The hunter was looking for _____ .
5. True or False: The hunter got the animal he wanted.

Hunting

My Dad and I go hunting.

We go hunting for deer.

It rains hard.

I get my face wet.

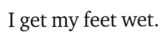

I get my feet wet.

We don't get no deer.

Level One   **Structured Stories**

Trouble

Vocabulary

Sight Words	Content Words
the	cops
came	house
not	Uncle
there	Arnie
they	trouble
want	

Already learned: to, my

You may substitute the word *policeman* for the word *cop. Cop* is much easier to read than *policeman,* however, and is more familiar to many students. Talk about the feelings of the writer when the policemen visited.

Content Questions
1. Arnie was not the writer's father. He was his _____.
2. The cops (policemen) came to the writer's house because _____.
3. The (cops) policemen left the writer's house because _____.
4. The writer thought Arnie was in _____ because the cops (policemen) came to find him.
5. True or False: The cops (policemen) came to arrest the writer.

Trouble

The cops came to my house.

They wanted Uncle Arnie.

Arnie is not here.

Arnie must be in trouble.

Level One   *Structured Stories*

What I Hear

Vocabulary

Sight Words	Content Words
what	sounds
hear	fire
if	ice cream
many	start(ing)
	cry(ing)
	bird(s)
	sing(ing)
	baby
	bell

Already learned: want, I, a, on, the, do, not

Note that many of the new content words have /ing/ endings. The sentence structure is repeated over and over: "I hear a _____." Talk about the tense being in the present. See if the students can remember the things that are heard.

Content Questions
1. The man driving the ice cream truck said _____ to the writer.
2- 5. Name four things that the writer heard:

What I Hear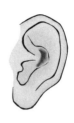

I hear a bird singing.

I hear a fire truck.

I hear a car starting.

I hear a baby crying.

I hear the bell on the ice cream truck.

I run to the ice cream truck.

I hear the ice cream man say, "Want ice cream?

I say, "Yes!"

Level One   **Structured Stories**

Hot

Vocabulary

Sight Words	Content Words	
very	July	hot
outside	Mom	hat
am	sun	keep
her	nothing	mow
then	lawn	cool(er)
off	finish	water
	turn(s)	hose
	bucket	anymore

Already learned: Dad, I, it, is, get(s), big, to, face, me, of, on, we

The sentences in *Hot* are mostly short. The situation itself is quite simple, so the student should be able to learn more of the content words easily. The two dunking events at the end give an amusing twist to the story.

Content Questions
1. Dad was hot, so he got himself a _____.
2. Mom was hot so she got herself a _____.
3. I was hot, so I got _____.
4. Dad played a joke on the writer by _____.
5. The writer paid Dad back by _____.

Hot

It is July and it is very hot outside.

The sun is bright and there are no clouds in the sky.

My family is outdoors in the yard this morning.

My Dad and my Mom are hot.

I am really, really hot!

My Dad gets a big fan.

The fan keeps him cool.

Mom gets a hat.

She is cooler.

I get nothing!

I get to mow the lawn.

It is a hot job, but I do finish.

My Dad gets the water hose.

He sprays me with water.

I'm going to get him back.

I fill a bucket with water.

Then I get Dad wet—really wet!

I am not hot anymore!

Rain Plus

Vocabulary

Sight Words	Content Words	
saw	watch(ing)	TV
over	thunder	lightning
heard	lights	dark
off	afraid	Fred
where	hiding	paws
his	ears	bark
was	porch	plus
	back	suddenly

Already learned: to, the, a, he, my, goes, is, of, too, am, we, I, on, he, has, off, rain, happy, street, turn

    Ask the students if they have had experiences with lightning and bad storms. Has the power gone out at their home? See if they have dogs. Are their animals afraid of storms? You want them to identify with the people in the story.

Content Questions
1. The TV went off because _____.
2. The dog Fred was afraid of _____.
3. The writer went to the _____ to find his dog.
4. The writer knew his dog was afraid because he _____.
5. At the end of the story, Fred was _____.

Rain Plus

I was watching TV.

I heard thunder.

I saw lightning.

I heard the rain . . . lots of rain.

Suddenly the TV turned off.

The lights in the house turned off.

The lights on the street turned off.

Where was my dog Fred?

He is afraid of rain.

I went to my porch.

Fred was hiding.

He had his paws over his ears.

Suddenly the lights came back on.

Fred barked a happy bark. I was happy too.

Level One   Structured Stories

Swim

Vocabulary

Sight Words	Content Words	
went	swam	round
with	center	lazy
around	river	time
help	fast	move(d)
could	yell(ed)	three
that	water	call(ed)

Already learned: to, the, a, and, of, me, not, with, on, was, my, go(es), one, is, it, get, all

This story has some words that add /ed/ to make the past tense. Do not try to teach the past tense of swim as *swam*. Just teach *swam* as a content word. Irregular past tenses are considered a more difficult topic for this group.

Content Questions
1. The Swim Center has _____ pools.
2. The pool that has water going round and round is called the _____.
3. The writer had a problem when it was time to go home. _____.
4. The person who helped the writer was _____.
5. The writer went swimming at the _____.

Swim

I went to the Swim Center. The Swim Center has three pools.

One pool is round. It is called the Lazy River. The water in the pool goes around and around.

I swam and swam and swam on the Lazy River.

Then it was time to go home.

I could not get out of the pool.

The water moved me around and around—fast.

Help," I yelled.

My friend pulled me out of the water.

That Lazy River was *not* lazy with me!

The Sandwich

Vocabulary

Sight Words	Content Words
can too	put each sandwich mouth big

Already learned: I, want, a, the, for, my, it, is

You can see how the sentences repeat themselves. Once they are learned, the student feels success. Point out the words describing the pictures, even if the student doesn't have to learn them in this lesson.

You can make a sandwich as described in the story with the students as a concrete illustration associating reading with good food. You may want to give the students the option of leaving out one ingredient.

The Sandwich (#1)

I want a 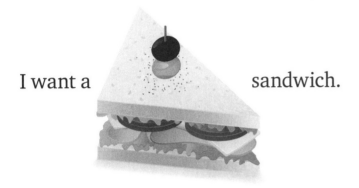 sandwich.

I put  on the sandwich.

I put 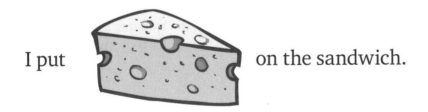 on the sandwich.

I put a  on the sandwich.

I put  on the sandwich.

I put  on the sandwich.

I put  on the sandwich.

I put a  on the sandwich.

I put a  on the sandwich.

I can't eat the sandwich.

It is too big for my mouth.

Level Two Structured Stories

The structured stories in Level Two are longer than those in Level One. Students are expected to learn more words for each story in Level Two. With each successive story, the sight words build on those taught previously, so it is better to read each story in the order given. However, if the stories are not read in order, the teacher should pre-teach the words that the student does not know.

At this point, the teacher should probably begin keeping a record of the sight words and content words that have been introduced to each student, and indicate when each word is mastered. One way to do this is to keep a simple list of words in the student's notebook and check them off as they are learned. Show the record to the student frequently so she can keep track of her own progress.

Sight Words	Content Words
are ✔	sandwich ✔
it ✔	ham
to	jam

Level Two   **Structured Stories**

The Sandwich

Vocabulary

Sight Words	Content Words
can too	ham cheese pickle lettuce peanut butter jam tomato banana

Already learned: a, we, of, my, me, was, and, I, am, the, can't, sandwich, mouth, big, it

This story also appears in Level One. At Level Two, however, the student is expected to read the words for the ingredients, rather than being cued by pictures. Note: When you first read the story, cover the pictures with a piece of paper to make sure the student can read the words for the foods.

Content Questions
1–5. Name the food items that were put on the sandwich. See if the students can repeat the items in the order they were given.

The Sandwich (#2)

I want a sandwich.

I put ham on the sandwich.

I put cheese on the sandwich.

I put a tomato on the sandwich.

I put lettuce on the sandwich.

I put peanut butter on the sandwich.

I put jelly/jam on the sandwich.

I put a pickle on the sandwich.

I put a banana on the sandwich.

I can't eat the sandwich.

It is too big for my mouth.

Level Two   *Structured Stories*

Daniel

Vocabulary

Sight Words	Content Words	
best likely	Daniel practice draw(ing) basketball character(s) odd Kris Tal Blux Walsh	art practice sketch(es) figure Chad Leeka tall shy

    This structured story is a student's language experience story. If you wish, you can change the names of Daniel's characters, if you think they are too difficult for your older students. Daniel is imaginative in inventing names of both people and places. Look at the characters he drew for the book. You may want to use his story as an example to illustrate drawing pictures for a language experience story.

Content Questions

1–2. Name two of the characters that Daniel drew.

3–4. Where does Daniel think that his friends (characters) would likely go?

5. What materials does Daniel use for his drawings?

Daniel

My name is Daniel. I like art. I practice drawing my sketches.
I like to draw characters I make up in my head.

One of my characters is a football player, and he is good at art.
His name is Chad Leeka. He is sometimes the odd ball. He likes math and stuff.

His best friend is very smart, but he is very shy. His friend's name is Kris Tal.

Another kid is very tall, so he is the best basketball player at this school. His name is Blux Walsh.

When I think about my characters, I start to sketch them. Then I can figure out what they would most likely do.

Maybe they will go to a fast food place called Shiver Malt.

Maybe they will go to the Zach Cinema to see a movie.

I like drawing them whenever I have free time. They are usually pencil and paper drawings.

How We Got the Ohio River
A Folk Tale

Vocabulary

Sight Words	Content Words		
how	wolf	sun	shade
enough	creek	deep(er)	end(ed)
still	hard	sudden	animals
so	beautiful	water	Ohio
became	bright	cloud	downhard
day	feet	stop(ped)	land tree
ran	rising	climb(ed)	

Already learned: to, the, but, that, does, and, walk(ing), went, like, am, not, my, was, couldn't, is, me, good, he, it, very, said, made, hot, happy, more, big, ran, this, around, some, rain, fast

You can see a pattern in this folk tale. The wolf wants something; he gets it, but then he is not happy. He wants more. This pattern repeats several times. The story also has the moral of not asking for too much. This tale is in a genre different from the previous stories based on language experience stories.

By the time the student is at Level 2, he may be able to answer questions that are written with /wh/ words in question word order. You can change these content questions if you are sure the student understands the question.

Content Questions
1. Wolf went walking and he felt very _____.
2. The first thing the Wolf asked for was _____.
3. Then the Wolf was not happy and he asked for more _____ .
4. Secondly, the Wolf asked for different weather, which was _____.
5. Too much water made a _____.

How We Got the Ohio River
A Folk Tale

One day, Wolf was walking.

The sun was very bright and Wolf was very hot.

"I want a cloud," Wolf said.

So a cloud came and made some shade for Wolf.

But Wolf was not happy.

"I want more clouds," he said. More clouds came.
But Wolf was still hot.

"I want rain." said Wolf. The rain came.
But Wolf was still not happy.

"I want more rain," Wolf said.
The rain came down hard and fast.
But Wolf was not happy.

"I want a creek to put my feet in," said Wolf. So a creek came.
The water ran in the creek. Wolf walked in it.
But Wolf was not happy.

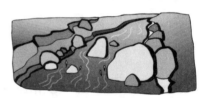

"I want it to be deeper," said Wolf. The creek became a deep river. All of a sudden,
Wolf fell in the river.

"Stop, stop! This river is big enough," said Wolf. The river stopped rising. Wolf climbed out of the river.

Other animals came to drink at the river. Trees grew up along the river. The land around the river became very beautiful.

And that is how we got the Ohio River.

Level Two **Structured Stories**

Summer Camp

Vocabulary

Sight Words	Content Words		
said	football	aunt	Brett
than	Ben	Rose	year
younger	saved	mother	class
as	camp	arts	trouble
all	breathe	learn	head
better	help(ed)	summer	glad
	cousin		

Already learned: to, the, but, that, does, and, that, walk, went, like, am, not, my, was, could, is, me, good, he, me, it, baby, friend

Content Questions

1. The writer did not want to go to the camp where Brett was going because _____.
2. The writer wanted to go to a _____ camp.
3–4. Brett's camp had classes in _____ and _____.
5. Brett helped the writer by _____.

Summer Camp

"But I do not want to go to that baby camp," I said to my mother.

"My friend Ben is going to football camp."

"That camp just does arts and swimming."

Mom said, "Aunt Rose needs you to go to that camp with your cousin Brett.

He needs a friend at camp."

I like Brett all right, but he is three years younger than I am.

So I went to camp with Brett. I went to art class. I went to swimming class.

I am not very good at swimming!

One day, I hit my head as I was swimming.

I couldn't breathe.

Brett jumped in the water, and he saved me. He is a good swimmer.

After that day, Brett went to swimming class with me.

Brett helped me really learn to swim.

I am glad I learned to swim better.

It was good that I went to that "baby camp" with Brett.

Level Two   **Structured Stories**

Brownies

Vocabulary

Sight Words	Content Words	
out	need	stir
measure(ing)	stuff	brownie(s)
oh	bowl	mix
	oven	open
	oil	pan
	water	spoon
	cup	forgot
	pan	

Already learned: eat, I, a, it, put, get, in

In case you want to bake these brownies, you need 3 tablespoons of oil and 2 tablespoons of water. You can use the oil bottle, the water, the brownie mix, the bowl, and the measuring spoons as visual aids. Put the items in front of the students. Ask them each to read a line and act it out with the items

Content Questions

1. The writer forgot to put a _____ on the table.
2–5. Name four of the ingredients needed for the brownies.

Brownies

I want brownies.

I need water, brownie mix, oil, a bowl, measuring spoons, and cups.

I open the mix.

I put it in a bowl.

I put oil in the bowl.

I put water in the bowl.

I stir and stir all the stuff.

I pour the stuff in a baking pan.

Oh, I forgot to get out a baking pan!

I put the baking pan in the oven.

I eat brownies.

Level Two   **Structured Stories**

The Big Snow Storm

Vocabulary

Sight Words	Content Words		
into	children	snow	lot
was	job	freeze(ing)	rain
were	ice	friend(s)	storm
also	week	plows (plowing)	finish(ed)
just	inside	hard(er)	happy
lot	outside	dress(ed)	slippery
but	sled	ride(ing)	last
then	heat	fill(ed)	close(d)
	school	people	turn(ed)
	fell	inside	now
	warm(ly)	cold	pile(d)
	street(s)	fireplace	

Already learned: big, we, a, my, of, it, not, me, on, and, the, but, they, in, went

Notice that the sentences are longer in this story. However, many of them are just short sentences connected by *and* or *but*. There are also some introductory clauses such as "When the snow plows finished plowing the streets...." Note that the story is longer than previous stories, so it may take longer for students to learn the vocabulary words.

Content Questions
1. The school was closed because _____.
2. The writer's job closed because _____.
3. _____ fell on the ice.
4 -5. Two types of weather told about in this story are _____ .

The Big Snow Storm

Last week we got a big snow storm.

We got a lot of snow on the streets.

The snow plows finished plowing the streets.

But then it just snowed harder and filled them up again.

My job was closed and my friends' jobs were closed.

The school was closed, but the children were happy. They went sled riding.

Many people lost power, and they had no heat in their houses.

Some of them had no water.

Then we got freezing rain, and it turned into ice.

My friends and I went outside. We dressed warmly, but we were all cold.

My friends fell on the slippery ice.

Not me!

We went inside my home, and then we were warm. We have a fireplace.

Level Two   **Structured Stories**

Shark

Vocabulary

Sight Words	Content Words		
likes	sea	fish(ing)	boat
every	hard	arm	nose
really	pull(ed)	broken	bandages
away	fix(ed)	weekday	nose
did	shark	doctor	bit
again	hurt	open(ed)	quickly
two	bone	cast	month(s)
	long		

Already learned: and, one, to, the, a, he, my, goes, is, of, too, am, we, I, on, has, was, off, in, that, day, time, mouth, could, time, day, hit, took, his

Sharks have a power of fascination for many people. You can often motivate a reader by having her illustrate the shark attack with a drawing.

Content Questions
1. The shark _____ Allen.
2–3. For two months, Allen couldn't _____ or _____.
4–5. Allen got away from the shark by _____.

Shark

Allen likes the sea and he likes to dive.

He likes to dive and see the fish in the sea.

Every weekday he swims in the sea.

One day he saw a shark in the sea.

Allen was afraid of the shark.

The shark hit Allen—hard.

The shark bit his arm.

That really hurt.

Allen hit the shark on the nose.

The shark opened his mouth.

Allen got his arm away from the shark.

A boat quickly came to Allen's side.

The men pulled Allen into the boat.

The men in the boat took Allen to the doctor.

The doctor fixed Allen's arm.

He fixed the broken bone in Allen's arm.

He put bandages and a cast on Allen's arm.

Allen could not get his arm wet for two months. He couldn't swim in the sea for two months.

Allen did not go swimming in the sea again for a long time!

Level Two   **Structured Stories**

Coming Through

Vocabulary

Sight Words	Content Words		
live(d)	through	wooden	cardboard
coming	floor	step(ped)	strong
own	roommates	hugged	hide
new	hall	fall	body
below	attic	hold	hang(ing)
look	Pam	ceiling	stuck
	hole	parents'	legs
	top		

This story has a simple plot with a beginning, several events, and an ending. It is about the kinds of experiences that older students can imagine. The illustrations add to the understanding of the story.

Content Questions
1. Pam and the writer were _____. They lived in the same house.
2. Pam wanted to hide in the _____.
3–4. Pam fell through _____. She didn't know that _____.
5. Pam was rescued by her _____.

Coming Through

Pam and I are friends.

Pam and I wanted to live in a house of our own as roommates.

We went to look at a new house. We liked the house, so we moved in.

One day Pam wanted to hide from me. She went into the attic of our new house.

At her parents' home, the attic had a wooden floor. She could walk on it.

The attic in the new house does not have a wooden floor. It has a cardboard floor.

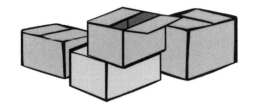

Pam stepped on the attic floor in the new house. The floor was not strong enough to hold Pam. Pam fell through the cardboard.

She did not fall all the way to the hall floor below.

She was stuck with the top of her body in the attic. Her legs were hanging from the hall ceiling. **She was STUCK!** She couldn't get up or down.

"Help!" Pam yelled at me.

"What are you doing?" I said.

"I am coming through," said Pam. "I am coming through."

Just then, Pam's father came to the new house.

He got Pam out of the hole in the ceiling.

Pam hugged her father and said to me, "I told you that I was coming through— and I did!"

Level Three

Level Three stories in the Triangle Approach use more compound words, contractions (*couldn't*), words with suffixes, and clauses than Level Two stories do. The sentences are also longer, and the stories overall are longer than Level Two stories and have more complex plots. There are usually more characters and conversation in Level Three stories than in lower level stories. The print size can be smaller than in Levels One and Two (12 point type is used here). However, there should be more white space between lines than is usual in commercial books.

In Level Three stories, the words that students have already learned are not listed as they are in Level One and Two. At this point, students probably have too large a reading vocabulary to list the words they know in every story. If the student misses a word that has already been introduced in previous stories, make a flashcard or word football of the word and re-teach it.

Level Three   **Structured Stories**

My Alien Friend

Vocabulary

Sight Words	Content Words		
from	scary	Jamal	fun
doesn't	bowl	basketball	move
	Mars	court	alien
	space	mission	land(ed)
	lunch	sorry	homesick
	green	Daniel	skin
	wrinkly	nice	

At this point, reading an imaginative science fiction story requires more skill than reading a story of a student's possible experiences. It is not as predictable as a lower level story. The print is smaller than for Level Two stories, but the surrounding white space is still very important.

Content Questions

1. Where did the alien first appear?
2. He crashed through the _____.
3–4. Describe the alien:

_____

_____

5. Why did the alien leave?

My Alien Friend

I was in a food court when an alien fell from space.

He crashed through the ceiling.

The alien landed on my lunch.
He said, "Sorry, I will buy you a lunch."

He was green and ten feet tall.
His skin was wrinkly. He was nice inside, but he looked scary.

I said, "My name is Jamal."
He said, "My name is 72394."

What can an alien and I do for fun?
He doesn't bowl, or ride a bike, or play basketball.

We went to a movie named Mission to Mars.

After the movie, 72394 got homesick.
So he went home.

Level Three   **Structured Stories**

Hidden

Vocabulary

Sight Words	Content Words		
finally	soldier	bike	woods
somewhere	met	something	stick(ing)
near	town	dug	box
still	rocket	bullet	explode(d)
however	explosive	light (lit)	found
maybe	body	ground	mad
against	sneak(ed)	tell	careful
sometime	fight(ing)	dangerous	bury(ied)
	rode	glad	scar
	dumb	bet	dare
	sweater	underarm	hid, hidden
	closet	lucky	tears
	stay	alive	burn(ed)

Hidden is set in post-World War II Germany, a time period that is not familiar to many students. The words may not even be in the student's spoken vocabulary. Some of the students may see it as an exciting adventure. I would relate the story to more recent conflicts and discuss the implications of post-war activities. It may be news to the students that people lived ordinary lives during and after wars

Content Questions
1. _____ was hidden in this story.
2. Heinz's mother said, "Don't go in the _____.
3. Heinz's mother knew he was burned because _____.
4. True or False: Heinz told his mother about the burn as soon as he got home.
5. True or False: Heinz did a dangerous and dumb thing.

Hidden

Sometime ago, it was spring in Germany. The soldiers were gone and the fighting was over. "I can finally go somewhere on my bike," Heinz said.

His mother said, "Be careful. Don't go near the woods. There may be dangerous stuff still buried out there."

Heinz met some of his friends, and they rode their bikes around the town.
Then they rode near the woods.

Heinz saw something sticking out of the ground. "Look! What is that?" he said. The boys got off their bikes and dug in the ground. They found a wooden box buried in the ground. They opened the box.

The soldiers had buried the box. There were explosives in it. Heinz said, "They are so big. They are much bigger than bullets."

One of his friends said, "Maybe they are for a rocket."

"No!" said Pete, the oldest of Heinz's friends. Pete grabbed one of the "bullets" and hit the end against a tree. Everyone jumped back. Nothing exploded, but the end fell off.
"I bet it will explode if we light it," Heinz said.

Pete said, "I dare you to do it."

So Heinz lit the explosive. (What a dumb thing to do!) Something hot and sharp from the explosive hit Heinz under his arm. He closed his arm against his body. Then it really hurt. It burned through his sweater.

As Heinz rode home on his bike, he thought about his mother. She was going to be mad!
He sneaked in his house and hid the sweater in the back of his closet.
His underarm was burned. It really hurt, but he didn't tell his family about the burn.

However, the sweater did not stay hidden. Heinz's mother found it in his closet.
She was really mad! His mother cried, "You could have been killed! You are lucky to be alive!
I can't believe that you would do something that dumb!"

Tears ran down his mother's face. Heinz cried too.

Heinz has a big scar under his arm from the burn. He couldn't use his bike for months, but both Heinz and his family are glad he is still alive.

Magic Under Ice

Vocabulary

Sight Words	Content Words
under air any minute	lock magician cut little between handcuffs Harry Houdini magic carry (carried)

This story has several long sentences and is about events that are probably not in the student's experience. Although the story has a simple plot and is somewhat predictable, there is a "twist" to the ending. It is like the kinds of stories that students read in the general curriculum.

Content Questions
1. What was Houdini's profession?
2. What was Houdini's first name?
3. Houdini wanted to do a special stunt in this story. What was it?
4. How did Houdini survive so long under the ice?
5. Have you ever seen a magician in person? Tell about it.

Magic Under Ice

Harry Houdini was a magician. He could open any lock.

He could open any handcuffs. He could open handcuffs under water.
He wanted to open his handcuffs under the ice.

One day, as a big crowd watched, they cut a hole in the ice.

They put handcuffs on Houdini. Houdini went down under the ice.

2 minutes

3 minutes

4 minutes

6 minutes

Houdini did not come up!

How could Houdini survive that long under water?

Then Houdini came up.

How did he survive under the water and ice???

Houdini got out of the handcuffs fast, but the water carried him away from the hole in the ice. He couldn't break through the ice. He knew there was a little air between the water and the ice. He used that air to swim back to the hole in the ice.

The crowd thought Houdini used magic to survive. But he really used his head!

Level Three   **Structured Stories**

Speed Demon

Vocabulary

Sight Words	Content Words		
been	travel(ing)	ski resort	mountain
during	part(s)	idea	alpine slide
might	reach bottom	park	chairlift
behind	skiers	car	winding
	cool	waiting	great
	beginning	wheels	forward
	left	right	straight
	curve	control	end

There are many words in this story that are specific to recreation (skiing, alpine slides). If your students don't have experience with winter sports, find some books that have good pictures of winter and sports. If the students do not relate to this story, make up a language experience story about something else that is familiar. Try to make it a two-page story.

Content Questions
1. Why was Ryan bored?
2. What was the country going to be like ahead of them?
3. What is an alpine slide?
4. How did people travel down the slide at the ski resort?
5. Who raced down the slide the fastest?

Speed Demon

Ryan's family was driving home after their vacation. Ryan was bored.
He had been traveling in the car for the last four days.

His mother said, "In the winter time, there is a ski resort in the mountains here."
She pulled out a travel book. "I have an idea. Let's go to the ski resort and see if they have an alpine slide during the summer."

"We can't ski now in the summer," said Ryan.

His mother said, "You ride up the mountain on a chairlift just like the skiers do.
Then they have a long winding slide that you ride down the mountain."

"How?" Ryan said.

"They have a cart that you ride on," said his mother. "You push on a handle that makes it go faster or slower."

"Well, that might be fun," Ryan said.

So the family drove to the ski resort. Just as they parked the car, it started to rain.
Not just a little rain, but a real cloudburst. No one could ride the lift or slide down the mountain during the rain.

Ryan's family sat in the car and waited. Finally the rain stopped.

The alpine slide opened up again. The family climbed up to the beginning of the chairlift. It was cool to see the tops of the trees as the chair went up the mountain.

They got off at the top of the mountain. There were two alpine slides winding around and down the mountain.

Ryan and his mother and father each got a cart. The carts have wheels. If you push forward on the handle, the wheels pull up and the cart goes very fast down the slide. If you pull the handle back, the cart slows down.

Ryan went on the left slide and pulled himself up to the starting point. His mother started on the right slide, but she was behind Ryan in starting.

Ryan started very fast, but he went very high on the first curve, so he slowed down to control his cart. He tried going slower as he went into the curve and then going faster as he went down the straight parts of the slide. He was having a great time.

Ryan finally reached the end of the slide. Then he saw his mother at the bottom waiting for him! She had started way behind him. She must have gone really fast!

His mother was a speed demon!

Level Three   Structured Stories

My Skateboard

Vocabulary

Sight Words	Content Words
also	skateboard
best	favorite
	deck
	trick
	kick flips
	ollies
	bump(s)
	driveway
	crack
	flew

This short story introduces words that may be unfamiliar to the readers. The student should ask about the tricks—kick flips and ollies (if she is not already familiar with skateboard terms). Skateboarding could become a topic for a student report and set the stage for more research or interviews on the subject.

Content Questions
1. What is the deck of a skateboard?
2. What are ollies?
3. How did the writer fall off his skateboard?
4. Why did the writer go too fast?
5. What happened to the writer's first skateboard?

My Skateboard

My skateboard is my favorite thing.
The deck is the top of my skateboard.
I can do tricks on my skateboard.

I can do kick flips.

I can do ollies.

I can make my skateboard jump over bumps.

When I started skateboarding, my friend told me to go down my driveway.
My driveway is on a hill. I really didn't know how to ride, so when my board hit a crack,
I flew about 5 feet and landed on my side. It really hurt. Also my board broke.

I got a new skateboard.

My skateboard is the best there is.

Level Three   **Structured Stories**

Fishing

Vocabulary

Sight Words	Content Words		
because	own(ed)	ladder	garage
care	young(er)	Frisbee	throw(ing)
any	shook	try(ied)	search
everyone	high(est)	branch(es)	touch
outside	invisible	pole	love(d)
let's	place	hands	tree
either	climb	knock	quick
	angry	line	truth
	laugh(ed)	lost	didn't
	stick		

The longer length of this story and fewer pictures help students transition to higher level reading skills. There are quite a few new words in this story, but the story is in a familiar setting, and includes experiences that may be familiar to the students. There is a plot with several events and at least three characters are involved. Ask your student(s) why Paul didn't stay angry (which will require them to make an inference).

Content Questions
1. Scott was playing with his _____. (Answer can be Frisbee or a friend.)
2. Paul kept his fishing pole in the _____.
3. Scott tried to get the Frisbee out of the tree by _____.
4. Paul got the Frisbee out of the tree by _____.

Fishing

Paul owned a good fishing pole. He loved fishing with his Uncle Mike. Paul took good care of his fishing pole because Uncle Mike had given it to him. He had a place in the garage for the pole. He told everyone in his family to keep their hands off his fishing pole.

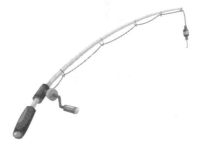

One day, Paul's younger brother Scott was playing outside with a friend. They were throwing a Frisbee. The Frisbee flew up in a tree and stuck there. Scott shook the tree to get the Frisbee down, but it didn't come down. Scott tried to climb the tree. He couldn't get up the tree. Then Scott's friend tried to get the Frisbee out of the tree, but he couldn't do it either.

Scott said that he needed a big stick to knock the Frisbee out of the tree. He went to the garage to search for a big stick. Then Scott saw Paul's fishing pole.

"That pole is long enough, but Paul will be mad at me. I will be quick and put it back."

Scott took the pole out of the garage. He used it to knock the highest branches of the tree where the Frisbee was stuck. The pole was not long enough. Scott pulled out the fishing line at the end of the pole. Then he threw out the fishing line as if he were fishing.

Just then Paul came running out of the house. He saw Scott with his fishing pole. He was very angry. "Put my pole down, Scott! You are not to touch my pole. What are you doing?"

Scott thought for a minute. Then he said, "I am fishing for invisible fish."

Paul yelled, "Invisible fish? Invisible fish?" Then Paul started to laugh. He laughed so hard that he just couldn't be angry any more. Then Scott and his friend started laughing too.

Paul said, "Now Scott, that isn't the truth, is it?"
Scott said, "My Frisbee is up in the tree."

Then Paul said, "I think I can help you." Paul got a ladder and climbed up into the tree. Paul threw the Frisbee down from the tree to Scott. Paul said, "Scott, when you have something lost up high, call me. I will help you."

Scott said, "Yeah."

Paul went inside the house saying to himself, "Invisible fish, invisible fish," and he laughed.

Level Three   Structured Stories

Glass

Vocabulary

Sight Words	Content Words		
once	king	kingdom	daughter
upon	marry	throne	glass
set	golden	disappear(ed)	lap
should	apple	invite(d)	horse
while	husband	duke	knight
	one	Alex	Grant
	order(ed)	fail(ed)	practice
	horseback	caught	half
	saddle	castle	exercise(d)
	yard	slid	count
	third(s)		

   Glass is a version of the Cinderella folk tale, focused on the man. Ask the students the reasons behind some of the very improbable events in the story. For example, why did the king set up the challenge? Why was it a glass hill? Why give the Princess three golden apples? Just because a man could ride a horse up a glass hill, would that make the man the right one to marry the king's daughter? You can also have the students compare *Glass* with Cinderella.

Content Questions
1. Why did the king put his daughter on the top of a glass hill?
2. Why didn't the people of the kingdom know who the man riding the black horse was?
3. Did Alex and Grant ride their horses up the glass hill?
4. Who was the man on the black horse really?
5. What did the Princess have on her lap?

Glass

Once upon a time, there was a king of a small kingdom who wanted his daughter to marry. He put his daughter upon a throne on the top of a glass hill. She had three golden apples in her lap.

The king invited all the men in the kingdom to ride a horse to the top of the glass hill and get an apple from the Princess. The first man to get an apple would marry the Princess.

The Duke called his two sons, Alex and Grant. "You should practice horseback riding so you can ride to the top of the glass hill. Go out to the stable and order the stable boy to saddle up your horses."

Alex and Grant went to the stable and ordered the stable boy to saddle their horses. The stable boy saddled the horses and Alex and Grant rode off. The stable boy then exercised the other horses. Every day Alex and Grant rode their horses while the stable boy rode the other horses around the exercise yard.

Finally the day came for the ride on the glass hill. Many men tried to ride up the glass hill, but the horses slid on the glass hill and couldn't get up. Alex and Grant also tried to ride up the hill, but they did not make it either.

Finally a knight on a large black horse rode his horse halfway up the hill. Then he turned his horse around and went back down the hill. The Princess threw a golden apple to him. The knight caught the apple and rode away.

The next week, the men of the kingdom tried again to climb the glass hill. No one could ride up it. When all the men had failed, the knight on the black horse rode two thirds of the way up the glass hill, then turned around and went back. The Princess threw down a second golden apple to the knight. The knight caught it and disappeared.

The next week, the Princess sat on the top of the glass hill, but none of the men of the kingdom wanted to try to ride. Finally the knight with the black horse came back and rode all the way up to the top of the hill. The Princess gave the last golden apple to him. The knight did not stop but went back down the other side of the hill and disappeared.

The king sent soldiers all through the kingdom looking for a man with a golden apple.

The soldiers came to the Duke's castle and asked to see Alex and Grant. Alex and Grant did not have the apple. The soldiers asked if there were any other men in the castle. "Only the stable boy," the Duke said.

Alex and Grant said, "Father . . . he doesn't count. He is only a stable boy."

The soldiers said that they must see the stable boy. "Do you have one golden apple?" they said.

"No. I don't have *one* golden apple! I have *three* golden apples," said the stable boy.

"Then you are the knight with the black horse," said the soldiers.

"Yes, I am Prince Glass, and I came to this kingdom so I could marry the Princess.

We will get married."

And they did.

Appendices

Appendix A: Teacher Materials

- A1—Story Forms
- A2—Vocabulary Words Forms (Footballs)
- A3—Fry's First 100 Sight Words

Appendix B: Student Materials

- B1—Letter Name Flashcards
- B2—Go Fish Rhyme Game
- B3—Letter Sounds Flashcards
- B4—Tower Consonant Game
- B5—Cube Game with Digraphs
- B6—Word Family Worksheets
- B7—Changing the Story
- B8—Silent E Bingo
- B9—Vowel Pairs Worksheet
- B10—Bing-o for Vowel Pairs
- B1—Worksheet on C
- B12 —Worksheet on G
- B13—C and G Memory Game
- B14—Blends Worksheet
- B15—Blends Memory Game
- B16—Tic Tac Toe Plurals
- B17—Past Tense Worksheet
- B18—Continuous Actions Worksheet
- B19—Tic Tac Toe Word Endings
- B20—R-Controlled Crossword Puzzle #1
- B21—R-Controlled Crossword Puzzle #2
- B22—Compound Words Game
- B23—Worksheet on Dividing Words into Syllables
- B24—Prefixes Worksheet
- B25—Suffixes Worksheet
- B26—Prefixes and Suffixes Crossword Puzzle
- B27—Match Game – Contractions
- B28—Worksheet on Dividing CVC Words
- B29 – Syllable Rules (Reference Sheet)
- B30 —Open and Closed Syllables (Reference Sheet)

A1

Experience Story Form

Title:

Author:

Describe the setting:

Activities:

Problem:

Outcome:

Sight Words	Content Words

A1

Sequence Story Form *(Making Something—recipes, objects, etc.)*

Title:

Author:

Setting:

Sequence:

Outcome:

Sight Words	Content Words

A1

Description Story Form *(person, animal, etc.)*

Title:

Author:

Identification:

Description:

Sum up:

Sight Words	Content Words

A2

Vocabulary Words Form *(Footballs)*

Story:

Author:

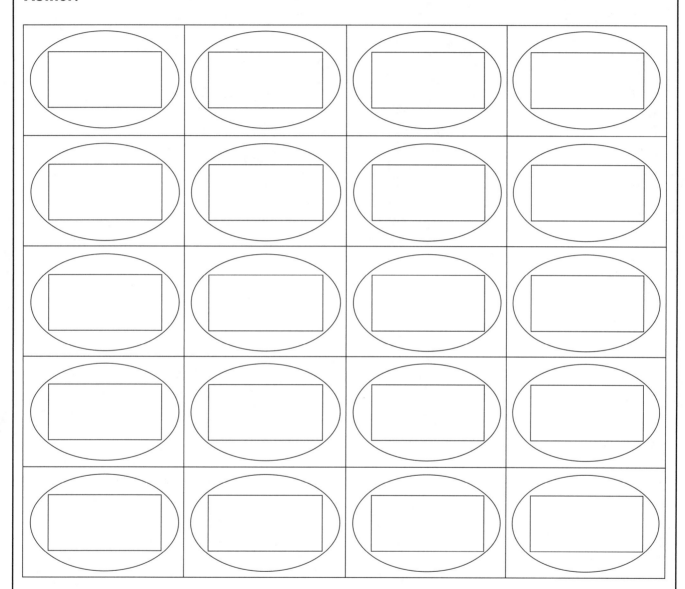

Type or print new or not-yet-learned words in the boxes and cut them out. Put words in a small, clear plastic bag and label with the name of the story. Throw the word squares onto a table or the floor, calling them footballs. Ask the student to pick up the words he or she knows and say them to you. Make two piles of words—correct and not correct. Review the incorrect words with the student. Show the student where the word is in the story. See if the student can read the words independently after the review.

Note: If you make two copies of the football sheet, you can use the copy to keep track of the vocabulary the student is learning instead of recording the words on the experience story form.

A3

Fry's First 100 Sight Words

Dr. Edward Fry updated the Dolch sight words to make a list of words that readers need to be able to read in order to be proficient. The first 100 words in order of their frequency make up approximately one-half of all of the words found in English language publications (Fry, 1994). These 100 words are listed here in alphabetical order so you can easily check which of the words the student has learned.

1. a	39. is	77. these
2. about	40. into	78. they
3. all	41. it	79. this
4. an	42. like	80. time
5. and	43. long	81. to
6. are	44. look	82. two
7. as	45. made	83. up
8. at	46. make	84. use
9. be	47. many	85. was
10. been	48. may	86. water
11. but	49. more	87. way
12. by	50. my	88. we
13. call	51. no	89. were
14. can	52. not	90. what
15. come	53. now	91. when
16. could	54. number	92. which
17. day	55. of	93. who
18. did	56. oil	94. will
19. do	57. on	95. with
20. down	58. one	96. word
21. each	59. or	97. would
22. find	60. other	98. write
23. first	61. out	99. you
24. for	62. over	100. your
25. from	63. part	
26. get	64. people	
27. go	65. said	
28. had	66. see	
29. has	67. she	
30. have	68. so	
31. he	69. some	
32. her	70. than	
33. him	71. that	
34. his	72. the	
35. how	73. their	
36. I	74. them	
37. if	75. then	
38. in	76. there	

B1

Letter Name Flashcards *(Front and Back)*

Cut out the cards so there is a picture on the left hand card and the corresponding letter and word on the right hand card. Fold the cards so the pictures are on the front and the letter and the word are on the back. You will then have a flashcard with a picture on one side and the letter-word on the back. You can also glue the backs of the picture cards to the backs of the letter-word cards to get the same effect. Mark the tops of the vowel flashcards with a colored mark at the top so you can see which ones are vowels when you glance at the card.

Consonants

	**b—ball**		**c—cat**
	**d—dog**		**f—fish**
	**g—girl**		**h—horn**
	**j—jet**		**k—king**

B1

	l—lip		m—man
	n—nest		p—pig
	q—queen		r—rain
	s—sun		t—tiger
	v—violin		w—worm

B1

	x—x-ray		**y—yarn**
	z—zipper		

Vowels

	A—apple—a		**E—egg—e**
	I—itch—i		**O—ox—o**
	U—up—u		**Y** at the end of a word when sounded like long /i/ or long /e/. cr**y**, pupp**y**

Note: say, "For Y at the end when it says eye or ee."

B2

Go Fish Rhyme Game

Cut out the rhyme cards. Give 5 cards to each player (including teacher). Place the rest of the cards face down in a pile on the table. The first player asks the next player if he or she has a card that rhymes with the card that he is showing. (The teacher should name the picture if the player does not know what it is.) If the second player has a rhyming card, it must be given to the first player. (Again, the teacher may need to look at the other player's cards to see if he or she has a match.) The first player puts down the rhyming pair on the table. The first player can then ask for a card to match another card in his hand. If the second player does not have a rhyming card, the first player takes a card from the pile in the center. The next player takes a turn. The player with the most rhyme pairs at the end of the time wins.

Since your students are older, they may notice that the matches end in the same letters. You can encourage this observation, but the purpose is really to *hear* the rhyming sounds.

| **hat** | **cat** | **man** |
| **can** | **sad** | **mad** |

B2

ham	jam	cap
map	nut	cut
sit	hit	lip

B2

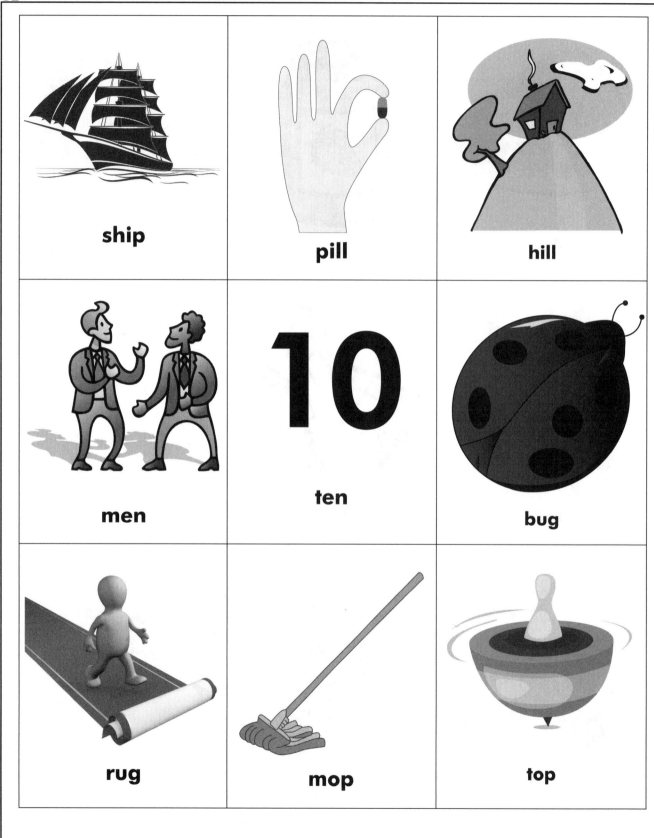

ship

pill

hill

men

ten

bug

rug

mop

top

B2

drum

gum

dog

frog

duck

truck

pin

win

sun

B2

run

B3

Letter Sounds Flashcards *(word and picture)*

Consonants

 **b—ball**	 **c—cat**
 **d—dog**	 **f—fish**
 **g—girl**	 **h—horn**
 **j—jet**	 **k—king**

B3

l—lip

m—man

n—nest

p—pig

q—queen

r—rain

s—sun

t—tiger

B3

v—violin

w—worm

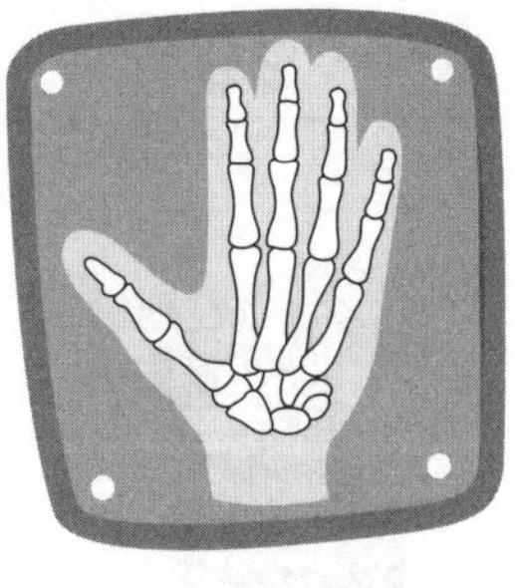

x—x-ray

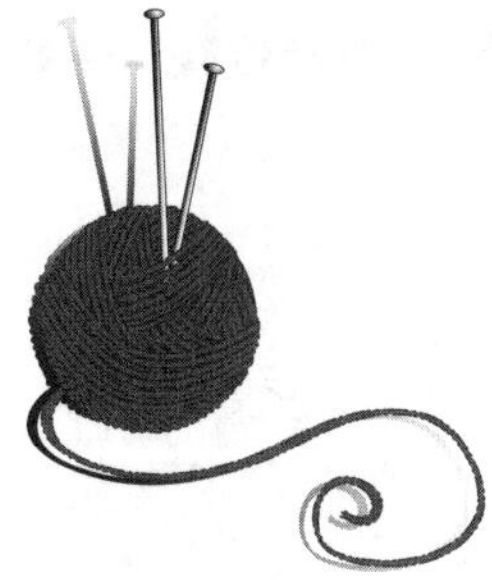

y—yarn

z—zipper

B3

Vowels

A—apple—a

E—egg—e

I—itch—i

O—ox—o

U—up—u

Y at the end of a word when sounded like long /i/ or long /e/. cr**y**, pupp**y**

B4

Tower Consonant Game

Cut out two towers for each student. If you have more than two students, photocopy the towers or print them out from the CD. You need only one set of the Tower cards. Place the cards face down in the middle of the game. Have the students look at the top picture on the flashcards. The student must pronounce the word and decide if it begins with the letter on the top of one of his towers. He or she puts the card on the floor of the correct tower. The teacher can give help at first and also correct mistakes. The student who finishes two (or one) tower(s) first is the winner.

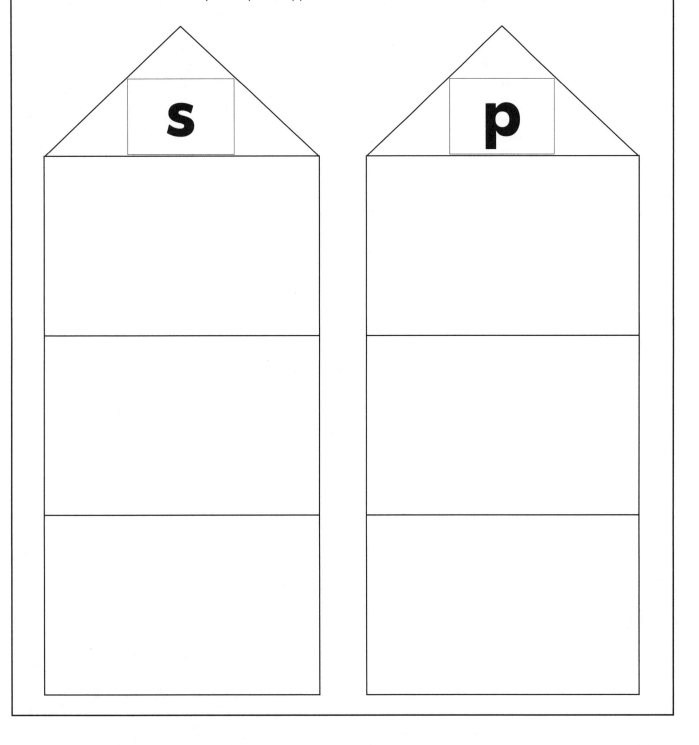

B4

You can make more towers by writing over the letters on the top of the towers and finding pictures or words starting with those letters. You can have the students find pictures starting with those letters.

Cut out squares and write in the letters you want your students to work on. Place at the top of the towers.

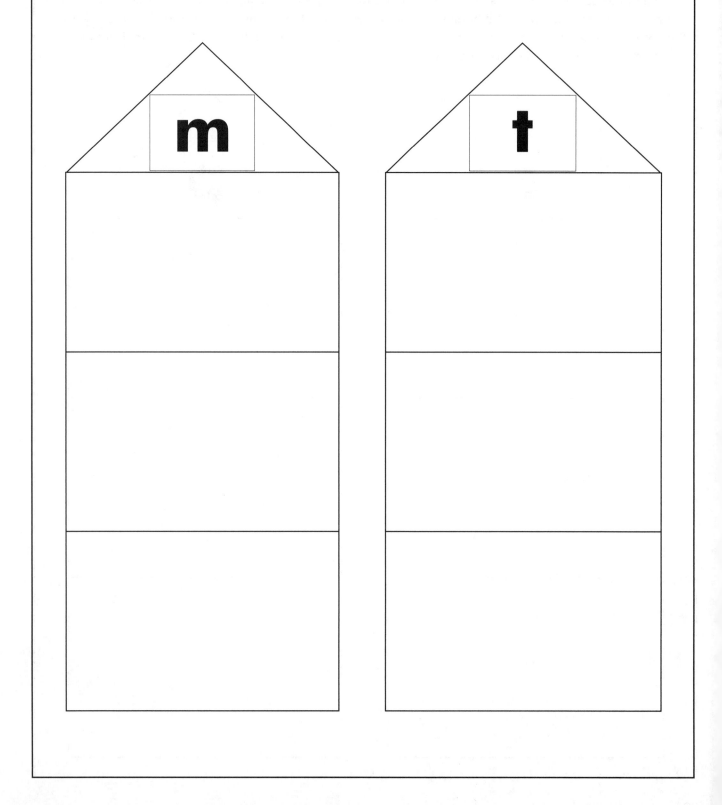

B4

B4

7	6	pet
table	meat	

B5

Cube Game with Digraphs

- If possible, copy the cube (below) on cardstock and cut out. Or paste it on index cards and cut out. Tape the cube together with transparent tape.
- Cut out the words on the accompanying pages and put them face up on the table.
- Have the student toss the cube. If a digraph is on top, the student must choose a word using that digraph. The student keeps that card. If the star is on top, he must choose a word without a digraph. If he is correct, he also keeps the card.
- The players take turns throwing the cube.
- If an appropriate card is not there, the player loses that turn and the next player continues.
- The winner is the one with the most cards when the time is up. (The teacher sets the time limit.)

Digraph Cube

*

CH   **SH**   **WH**   **TH**

*

B5

Making Digraphs

w	s	c	t	h
wh	sh	ch	th	h
h	h	h		

B5

Words with Digraphs

ouch	cherry	the	thing	white
wheel	thumb	fish	dish	ship
bath	math	chat	chop	rich
shell	whale	what	wheat	chip
march	shut	shop	thank	thin

Words Not Using Digraphs

mat	red	tree	dream	heat
water	look	hot	ham	jam
ball	doll	hill	book	poor
mom	table	ice	bug	tall

B6

Word Family Worksheets

Word Family /ap/

My name is Zap.

I fell into a trap.

I lost my cap.

Guess I will take a nap.

Circle the /ap/ in each of the following words:

nap	gap	tap	cap	lap
rap	map	trap	zap	

Word Family /an/

I look for my lizard Dan,

Is he under the can?

Is he under the pan?

No, away he ran.

Circle the /an/ in each of the following words:

Dan	fan	man	Jan	plan
pan	can	tan	ran	van

B6

Word Family /at/

Hey Pat,

You sat

On my hat,

Don't do that!

You'll get hit with a bat.

Circle the /at/ in each of the following words:

cat   fat   bat   rat   Pat

at   sat   mat   hat   that

Word Family /it/

Buying Shoes

Will it fit?

Just a bit?

If I sit?

Oh, I quit!

Circle the /it/ in each of the following words:

skit   it   bit   sit   kit

pit   mitt   hit   spit   quit

B6

Word Family /ip/

I dip,

    I flip,

        I slip.

            What a trip!

Circle the /ip/ in each of the following words:

rip	slip	nip	ship	tip
chip	flip	trip	drip	dip

Word Family /ig/

Bigwig.

    Captain Fig,

        Sailed a rig,

            Liked to dig,

                Found a pig,

                    Nicknamed Big.

Circle the /ig/ in each of the following words:

big	fig	rig	swig	pig
dig	gig	twig	wig	prig

B6

Word Families /ot/ and /op/

Scott got a pot.

The soup was hot.

He spilled a lot.

Here comes Pop.

He brings a mop.

Circle the /ot/ or /op/ in each of the following words:

cot	shop	mop	hot	stop
dot	pot	hog	drop	got

Word Families /ug/ and /uh/

Hug that bug,

Lug that mug,

Grab that jug

Pack that tub,

We're leaving, Bub.

Circle the /ub/ or /ug/ in each of the following words:

tub	bug	lug	sub	plug
jug	Bub	club	pub	hug

B6

Word Family /en/

When I count to ten,

My hen named Jen

Crows Amen.

Circle the /en/ in each of the following words:

hen	den	ten	amen	pen
men	Jen	wren	Ken	when

Word Family /et/

I bet,

You'll get wet,

My water cannon shoots a jet.

Circle the /et/ in each of the following words:

bet	wet	let	jet	yet
get	met	set	net	yet

B6

Word Family /ell/

I can tell,

    I can yell,

        I can ring a bell.

            Get rid of that smell!

Circle the /ell/ in each of the following words:

bell	tell	fell	well	swell
shell	yell	sell	smell	dell

B7

Changing the Story

My friend <u>Pete</u>   and I <u>made</u>   a trip to the <u>lake</u>   . We sailed on <u>Cane</u>   <u>Lake</u>   in an inner <u>tube</u>   . We fished. I got a <u>bite</u>   with my fishing <u>pole</u>   . The fish got away. That was <u>fine</u>   with me. The sun started to <u>fade</u>   from the sky. We saw a <u>huge</u>   black cloud. It started to rain. Pete said, "Hey, <u>dude</u>   . Do you want to <u>wade</u>   ?" We hurried <u>home</u>   . I <u>hope</u>   I get to go fishing again—but not in the rain!

B8

Silent E Bingo

Call List

This call list lists all the words on the cards in scrambled order. Just call them out one at a time, starting at the top. You can also give a clue rather than the word itself.

bake	cake	dive	rake
fill	none	ride	file
safe	time	hole	wake
fin	while	gate	whale
hid	bone	fine	life
hug	sale	huge	home
snake	date	fake	hide

B8

B	I	N	G	O
safe	hold	fine	bake	hide
none	wake	ride	date	rake
bone	fake	FREE SPACE	dive	home
while	gate	time	whale	huge
cake	snake	sale	file	life

B8

B	I	N	G	O
ride	huge	whale	cake	rake
none	life	fake	bone	time
date	file	FREE SPACE	while	gate
hide	dive	safe	bake	snake
hole	fine	wake	sale	home

B8

B	I	N	G	O
fine	life	rake	snake	none
huge	hide	hole	date	cake
fake	time	FREE SPACE	bone	safe
file	while	dive	ride	wake
whale	sale	bake	home	gate

B8

B	I	N	G	O
while	life	dive	ride	huge
snake	gate	cake	wake	fine
hide	time	FREE SPACE	file	bone
bake	sale	rake	date	fake
home	whale	safe	hole	none

B8

B	I	N	G	O
huge	file	hole	whale	bake
time	gate	dive	none	sale
rake	life	FREE SPACE	date	hide
while	safe	fake	home	fine
wake	bone	ride	cake	snake

B8

B	I	N	G	O
while	fine	bone	bake	time
hole	ride	hide	fake	none
gate	huge	**FREE SPACE**	wake	sale
file	date	safe	whale	snake
life	cake	home	rake	dive

B9

Vowel Pairs Worksheet

Rhyme:

When two vowels go walking,

the first one *usually* does the talking.

He says his alphabet name.

Unless he is an "outlaw," for shame.

- Have the students repeat the rhyme until it is memorized. (You may have them memorize just the first two lines.)
- Tell students that sometimes vowel pairs (for example, the word *said*) don't follow the rules. They are called "outlaws" in the Triangle Approach.
- **Cross out the silent letter and underline the letter that says its own name:**

c h a i n

Words with Vowel Pair /ai/

p a i l r a i n t a i l

m a i l t r a i n s a i l

Words with Vowel Pair /ea/

l e a f p e a c h s e a l

t e a t e a c h t e a m

Words with Vowel Pair /oa/

b o a t g o a t r o a d

t o a d c o a t s o a p

Words with Vowel Pair /ee/

f e e d m e e t b e e t

f e e t s h e e p f r e e

B10

Bing-o for Vowel Pairs

Cut out the following cards. Show the students each card as you pronounce the word. There are more words here than any one student will have on his or her card.

beach	eat	leaf	peach	sea	teach
beat	feet	lot	rain	sun	teeth
bee	fish	mail	road	sheep	table
coat	jail	meat	sail	soap	wait

1. Give each student a bingo card. The teacher will need to play if there is only one student.
2. Using the small teacher cards, show the students a card while you pronounce the name at least two times. There are words with long vowels, as well as words with short vowels for distracters. Have the students find the words on their bingo cards. Since a student has to scan 20 words when he or she looks for the named word, you may have two students work on one card at first. Beginning students may just have to tell whether the word has two vowels or one vowel to get a chip. The teacher or tutor will then point to the correct square so he or she can put down the chip.
3. Cover the named word with a bingo chip. Bing-o is called when a player covers a row or column or at least four words in a diagonal line.
4. Check the card to make sure the words are correct.

B10

B	I	N	G
rain	sun	table	mail
bee	sail	jail	peach
wait	lot	FREE SPACE	beat
eat	road	leaf	sea
meat	feet	teeth	soap

B10

B	I	N	G
sail	lot	beat	feet
meat	peach	soap	teeth
sheep	road	**FREE SPACE**	eat
sea	teach	wait	rain
beach	coat	mail	jail

B10

B	I	N	G
lot	sun	table	beach
jail	teeth	soap	eat
road	beat	FREE SPACE	wait
rain	fish	meat	bee
beach	coat	mail	jail

B11

Worksheet on C

1. Underline the C in each word.
2. Look at the vowel that comes after the C.
3. If the vowel is e, i, or y, the C is soft. You pronounce it like /s/ in sit.
4. If the vowel is a, o, or u, the C is hard. You pronounce it like /k/ in cat.
5. Write the sound for C after the written word—either K or S.

cat ___K___	catch _____	can _____	copy _____
cent _____	cell _____	cookie _____	city _____
come _____	could _____	coat _____	circus _____
call _____	cop _____	dance _____	fence _____

B12

Worksheet on G

1. Underline the G in each word.
2. Look at the vowel that comes after the G.
3. If the vowel is e, i, or y, the G is soft. You pronounce it like /j/ in gem.
4. If the vowel is a, o, or u, the G is hard. You pronounce it like /g/ in goat.
5. Write the sound for G after the written word—either J or G.

gas __G__	gym _____	gentle _____	giant _____
gold _____	girls _____	gallon _____	goose _____
giraffe _____	gym _____	bug _____	goal _____
garbage _____		orange _____	

B13

C and G Memory Game

- Cut out the C and G flashcards.
- Put the cards printed side down in three rows of six each.
- Have the student pick up and look at two cards. If the picture card matches the word card, the student keeps both cards. If there is no match, the student replaces both cards in the same place on the table. The next player continues, looking at two cards. Both players need to pay attention to where the cards are placed so they can make matches more easily.
- The player with the most matches at the end wins.

mice	goat	game
cake	gas	goose
clock	celery	cap

B14

Blends Worksheet

Circle the blend that starts the word that fits in the blank of the sentence. Many blends have an /r/, /l/, or /s/ in them. There are also three letter blends. Read the sentences to the students before they start their work.

1. When I am thirsty, I _____ a glass of water.   **dr**   or   **st**

2. When I get up from bed, I eat _____.   **pr**   or   **br**

3. I take an airplane when I _____to my grandpa's house.   **fl**   or   **gl**

4. At night I _____ in a bed.   **sl**   or   **tr**

5. I pour my orange juice into a _____.   **fr**   or   **gl**

6. At night we can see many _____ in the sky.   **st**   or   **cr**

7. A sign we often see on the street is a_____ sign   **st**   or   **pl**

8. At the baseball diamond, I _____ the ball to a friend. **cl**   or   **thr**

9. My friends brought _____ to my birthday party   **pr**   or   **dr**

10. I bought me an ice _____ cone.   **cr**   or   **sn**

11. The cars drive on the _____ in front of my house. **str** or   **fl**

12. We have a leafy oak _____ in our front yard.   **gr**   or   **tr**

13. We tell time by looking at the_____ on the wall.   **cl**   or   **st**

14. He was not a large dog. He was very _____.   **sm**   or   **fr**

15. He wore a uniform because he was a Boy _____.   **pl**   or   **sc**

16. When I am 16, I will learn to _____ a car.   **dr**   or   **bl**

17. I _____ some seeds in the dirt   **sn**   or   **pl**

18. In the winter time I often _____ on the ice.   **sk**   or   **gl**

19. The USA sent a rocket into outer _____.   **sp**   or   **gr**

20. My garden had three different kinds of pretty _____. **fl**   or   **st**

B15

C and G Memory Game

- Cut out the picture and blend cards.
- Put the cards printed side down in three rows of six each.
- Have the student pick up and look at two cards. If the picture card matches the word card, the student keeps both cards. If there is no match, the student replaces both cards in the same place on the table. The next player continues, looking at two cards. Both players need to pay attention to where the cards are placed so more matches can be made.
- Some pictures have the beginning letter on the card to help players with the label for the picture. (Some pictures can have different labels—e.g., the picture of fruit could also be interpreted as apple.)
- The player with the most matches at the end wins.

	g	p
Gr	Gl	Pl
Sp	Sch	St
Br	Fr	Bl

B16

Tic Tac Toe Plurals

- Cut out the word cards below and put in a hat or bowl, etc.
- Give each student (or student and teacher) a tic-tac-toe form.
- The players take turns pulling the singular words out of the hat or bowl (not looking at them before).
- The player then reads the word, pronounces the plural form, and, if correct, puts the word on his form on either a square with /s/ or /es/.
- The word in the middle of the form is an "outlaw" plural and the student must pronounce the plural correctly. If the student is incorrect, he puts the word square back in the hat/bowl and the next player draws a word.
- The first player to fill his whole form is the winner. (Or play until a certain number of squares are filled if you want a shorter game.) You can also make your own forms using the blank form in the appendix.

gas	dog	book	kiss	dish
girl	watch	apple	pear	glass
lake	box	deer	child	mouse
peach	man	tooth	boy	meat
fish	pencil	dress	cup	wax

B16

S	s	es
es	child	s
es	s	s

es	s	s
s	man	s
es	es	s

B16

es	s	es
s	tooth	es
s	es	s

s	es	es
s	mouse	s
es	s	s

B16

s	s	es
es	deer	s
es	s	s

B17

Past Tense Worksheet

Make the following verbs past tense (happening in the past):

1. work   _worked_

2. play   _____

3. run   _____

4. jump   _____

5. walk   _____

6. dress   _____

7. open   _____

8. cook   _____

9. move   _____

10. pull   _____

Make the following verbs present tense—no longer past tense.

11. voted   _vote_

12. painted   _____

13. loved   _____

14. helped   _____

15. danced   _____

16. chased   _____

17. shined   _____

18. rolled   _____

B18

Continuous Actions Worksheet *(present tense verbs with /ing/ endings)*

Add the /ing/ ending to the appropriate words. Cross out the silent e if it is not needed.

1. My aunt and uncle are (come) *ing* to visit.

2. I am not (go) _____ to that party.

3. The weather is so nice that I am (walk)_____ to school today.

4. The boys in the glee club are (sing)_____ in the program.

5. Alice is (live)_____ in Dublin.

6. Karl is (stand) _____ at the window.

7. His boss is (talk) _____ on the phone.

8. We are (travel)_____ to Florida.

9. I am (go) _____ to the swimming pool.

10. Ben is (try)_____ to fix his bike.

11. Teresa is (buy) ____ a pair of shoes.

12. Kayli is (bake) _____ cupcakes.

13. Paul is (sleep)_____ upstairs in his bedroom.

14. The dog is (bark)_____ all night long.

15. You are not (go)_____ out in the rain.

16. I am (watch)_____ TV.

17. We are not (work)_____ on Thanksgiving.

18. He is (smile) _____ at me.

19. Moira is (dry)____ her hair.

20. My friend is not (lose) _____ weight.

B19

Tic Tac Toe Word Endings

- Print out or copy the tic-tac-toe boards. Also cut out the sentence squares and put them in a bag or a bowl.
- The first student pulls a square out of the bag or bowl and reads the phrase with the correct ending. The teacher may help him read the phrase or the word.
- The student says the appropriate form of the word and puts the phrase square on his tic-tac-toe board on either /ing/ or /ed/ or /d/. If he is incorrect, he puts the phrase square back into the bag or bowl.
- The next student or the teacher pulls another square out and reads it. Then he says the appropriate form of the root word and tries to place it on the correct word-ending space on his board. The first player to fill his card wins. You can shorten the game by requiring a smaller number of squares to win. You can exchange game boards for a second round.

Note: See if your students can figure out that when there is a form of the verb to be (is, was, were, am, etc.), the action word following will take an /ing/ ending. Otherwise, the word will take an /ed/ or /d/ ending. Remind students that if the word ends with a silent /e/, you just add /d/.

Tic Tac Toe Word Endings Boards

ing	ed	ed
ing	d	ed
ed	ing	d

B19

ing	ed	d
ing	d	ing
ed	ed	d

ing	ed	d
ing	d	ing
ed	ed	d

B19

ed	ed	ing
ing	d	ed
ed	d	ing

d	ed	ing
ed	d	ing
ing	ed	ing

B19

ed	ing	d
ing	ed	ed
ed	ing	d

B19

Sentence Cards—Endings

Mark is (go)____ to help us.	I (play)____ the piano.	The frog (jump)____ over the rock.
Kyle is go____ to college.	Jake is (write)____ a book.	The boy (jump)____ over the fence.
I (hope)____ that I would be first.	I (lock)____ the door.	Alice is (brush)____ her hair.
Scott is (take)____ out the trash.	I (move)____ the boxes.	Every Monday I (walk)____ to the park.
My Dad is (work)____ at the gas station.	I (close)____ the door.	Steve (talk)____ too much.
Declan is (teach)____ at the school.	I (open)____ the door.	Scott (talk)____ fast.

Sentence Cards—Endings

She was (look)____ at the gas station	Karl (pack)____ his bag.	We (help)____ him pack.
Heather is (go)____ to meet us there.	I (play)____ the horn.	The driver is (drive)____ the truck.
We are (sing)____ a song.	He (use)____ the ladder.	Mom (bake)____ a cake.
Maria (cook)____ stew.	We (unlock)____ the door.	Rowan is (comb)____ her hair.
The cat (whine)____ over and over.	The teacher (reach)____ parking lot.	LaNell (sew)____ two pairs of pants.
He is (cough)____ all the time.	I am (wait)____ for my friend.	Katri (ski)____ down the mountain.

B20

R-Controlled Crossword Puzzle #1

Across:

3—Rain, thunder and lightning are part of a great _____.

4—He was _____ on the Fourth of July.

5—My hair is messy when I look in the _____.

7—He was _____ in line, not second.

8—The eight-year-old was in _____ grade.

Down:

1—I like _____ on the cob best.

2—After the rain, there were many _____s on the sidewalk.

3—She wore her new blouse and _____.

4—The farmer kept the cows in the _____.

6—He fell into a large pile of _____.

Possible Answers:

barn, born, corn, dirt, first, mirror, skirt, storm, third, worm

B20

R-Controlled Crossword Puzzle #1 Solution

B21

R-Controlled Crossword Puzzle #2

Across:

3—I ride every morning on my _____.

5—I put on my pants and my _____.

7—Bears have a _____ coat.

8—My mother says, "_____ off the TV."

9—The baby likes the pudding and says "Want _____."

Down:

1—I write with a pencil on _____.

2—Sue is a _____, not a boy.

3—If I fall, I may _____ myself.

4—It has feathers and flies. It is a _____.

5—At night I can see a _____ in the sky.

6—I drink 8 glasses of _____ a day.

7—I eat with a spoon and a _____.

Possible Answers:
bird, fork, fur, girl, horse, hurt, more, paper, shirt, star, turn, water

R-Controlled Crossword Puzzle #2 Solution

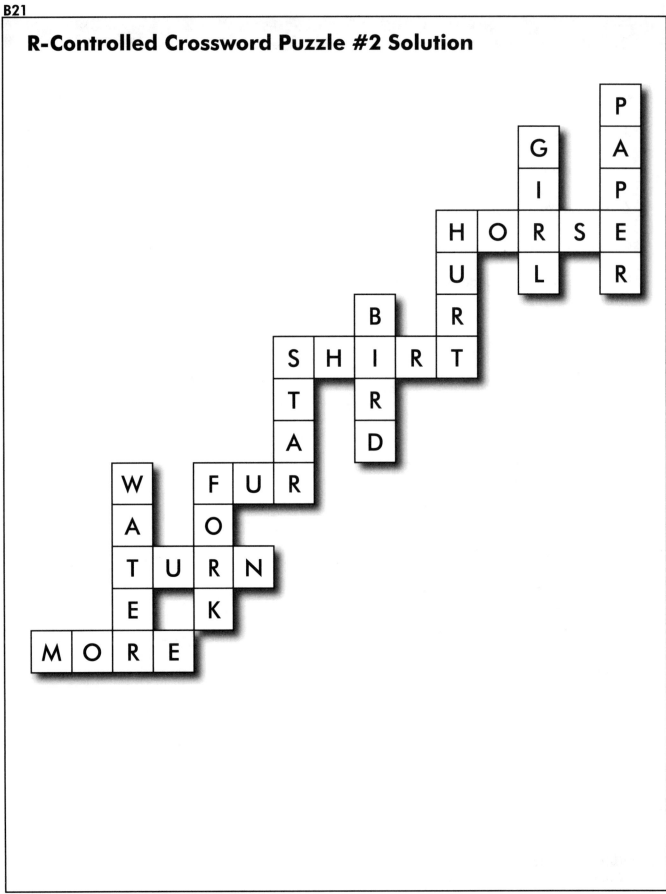

B22

Compound Words Game

Cut out the boxes. Start by handing out four compound words at a time. The students should be able to match up the 4 initial words with the 4 secondary words to make 4 real compound words. Later, hand out 8 or 12 initial and secondary words to make the task more difficult.

Initial	Second
apple	sauce
air	plane
sun	flower
blue	berry

Initial	Second
skate	board
some	thing
base	ball
out	side

Initial	Second
wheel	chair
camp	fire
sand	box
gold	fish

B23

Dividing Words into Syllables

Word	Reason	Word	Reason
little (lit/tle)	2 consonants	dinner (din/ner)	2 consonants
together (to/gether)	compound word	summer (sum/mer)	2 consonants
true		wishful	
football		number	
game		mother	
rabbit		safety	
purple		unit	
sleepy		bluebird	
lonely		help	
Kansas		circus	
moonlight		middle	
butter		candy	
sunny		monster	
corner		muffin	

B24

Prefixes Worksheet

No. of Syllables	Division	No. of Syllables	Division
_____ Return	re turn	_____ Rewrite	
_____ Depart		_____ Preview	
_____ Misfire		_____ Unhappy	
_____ Rerun		_____ Detour	
_____ Mistreat		_____ Disobey	
_____ Nonfat		_____ Mistake	
_____ Unclean		_____ Submarine	

Write the number of syllables in the words on the line. Write the word with the syllables separated. Discuss the meanings of the words using the chart below, if necessary.

Prefix	Meaning	Example	Prefix	Meaning	Example
Un	not	untie	Dis	not	disable
Pre	before	prepay	In, Im	not	imperfect
Re	again	replay	Sub	under	subway
Non	not	nonsense	Anti	against	antifreeze
Il, ir	not	illegal	De	opposite	defrost
Mis	not	misspell	Bi	two	bifocals

B25

Suffixes Worksheet

No. of Syllables	Underline suffix	Word	Underline suffix
____ careful	c a r e <u>f u l</u>	____ worker	
____ thirsty		____ retirement	
____ clueless		____ largest	
____ helpfully		____ tallest	
____ quickly		____ dirty	
____ government		____ going	
____ workable		____ baker	
____ waterless		____ artist	
____ formal		____ working	

Discuss the meanings of the above words. Use the chart below for meanings.

Suffix	Meaning	Example	Sufffix	Meaning	Example
er	worker of (or comparative)	farmer	tion, sion (pronounced shun)	act of	action
est	most	smallest	less	without	fearless
ful	full of	careful	ing	act of	going
able/ible	can be done	breakable	ly	characterisctic of	quickly
ment	act of	government	ful	full of	tearful
ness	state of	kindness	al/ial	having characteristic of	personal
y	full of	thirsty	ist	one who does	artist

B26

Prefixes and Suffixes Crossword Puzzle

Across:

5—On Thanksgiving day I am _____ for my food.

7—I tripped and _____ a whole glass of water.

8—Kayli was able to _____ her shoes.

10—Declan wanted to _____ his glass with juice.

Down:

1—My parents are my father and my _____.

2—Little Ben was the _____ of the brothers.

3—The kangaroo was _____ up and down.

4—I was walking and _____ on the way to school.

6—He goofed; he made a _____.

9—Rowan came early to the movie to see the _____s

Possible Answers:

refill, preview, thankful, mistake, untie, mother, spilled, jumping, running, smallest

Prefixes and Suffixes Crossword Puzzle Solution

B27

Match Game—Contractions

Cut out the following game cards. Mix them up and have the students match the contractions to their full forms.

They'll	They will	You're	You are
We've	We have	I'm	I am
We're	We are	She's	She is
You've	You have	I've	I have
We'd	We had or We would	Isn't	Is not
He's	He is	Mightn't	Might not
We'll	We will	That's	That is
Don't	Do not	Won't	Will not

B28

Worksheet on Dividing CVC Words

If the first vowel is long, the syllable divides after that vowel. If the first vowel is short, the syllable divides after the consonant. Put the following words under the **Spi der** rule if the vowel is long and under the **Cam el** rule if the vowel is short.

1. robin

2. lemon

3. final

4. siren

5. visit

6. token

7. salad

8. spiral

9. hazard

10. talent

11. novel

12. model

13. hazard

14. finish

15. limit

The Spider Rule and the Camel Rule

Spi der rule—divide after the vowel, making the vowel long (saying its alphabet name)

Cam el rule—divide after the consonant, making the vowel short.

B29

Syllable Rules *(Reference Sheet)*

1. **Every syllable has one vowel sound.** Remember that Y can be a vowel if it has the sound of long /e/ or /i/.

2. **A compound word is divided between the small words that make up the compound word:** cup / cake, base / ball, tooth / brush

3. **A prefix or suffix is a separate syllable:** re/main, un/ tie, care/less, farm/er.

4. **Separate 2 consonants in the middle of the word:** win/ter, fas/ter, gar/den, but/ter.

   Note: Do not separate consonant digraphs that have one sound (ch, sh, th, ph, wh) or blends such as bl, sk, cl, dr, and fl.

5. **A consonant in front of le makes a syllable:** ta/ble, cir/cle, bat/tle, pur/ple.

6. **When a vowel is sounded alone in a word, it forms a syllable by itself:** u /nit, A/pril, and ed/u/cation

B30

Open and Closed Syllables *(Reference Sheet)*

Closed Syllable

The vowel (girl) is <u>closed</u> in by a consonant (boy) on both sides. She can't run.
The vowel is ***short***.

If a syllable with a CVC pattern is **short**, it is a **closed syllable.**

Divide the word after the second consonant.

For example: **Cab**in. Divide after the second consonant (b)—cab / in

Remember, the vowel in a closed syllable is **short**.

Open Syllable

The vowel (girl) can run away because the consonant (boy) is only on one side.
The syllable is ***open***. The vowel is long (says its own name).

If a syllable with a CV (C or V) pattern is **long**, it is an **open syllable.**

Divide the word after the vowel.

For example: **Bas**ic. Divide after the vowel (A)—ba / sic

Remember, the vowel in an open syllable is **long**.

Resources

Many publishers publish books designed for older struggling readers that they call high interest-low vocabulary books. The books are usually written on a third- to fourth-grade level and will be useful for you after your student(s) has finished the exercises and activities in this book. We are therefore not listing high/low books here.

Beginning reading books are usually of two varieties. Books based on phonics are called *decodable.* Because the words are short and focus on one or two vowels or consonants, they are not very interesting. However, they can teach the phonics principles clearly. Books that are closer to children's literature, but are not phonics-based, are called *leveled* (or guided level) books. The higher a story's level, the more complex it is.

Free (Online) Books and Teaching Materials

- *Genie Books in Power Point: Decodable books for beginning readers*
  Price: Free
  www.auburn.edu/academic/education/reading_genie/bookindex.html
      Over 20 books written by Dr. Bruce Murray (the Reading Genie), an associate professor of Reading Education in the Department of Curriculum and Teaching at Auburn University. Some of the first stories may not be age-appropriate for secondary students; however, they do not seem "babyish." The site also has valuable information on teaching reading.

- *Easy Garfield Readers*—Professor Garfield Foundation (an educational collaboration be-tween Paws, Inc., the global headquarters for Garfield the Cat, and Ball State University)
  Price: Free (online)
  www.professorgarfield.org
      Games and stories for sight reading and phonics for early readers. The pictures are like the Garfield comics, but the narration may be condescending for older stu-

dents. Website is colorful and interesting and can be used to practice sight words in an engaging way. There are two versions of each story available. The first is unedited and can be used to gain familiarity with the text. The "altered version" gives students the ability to fill in the blank with the correct sight words. Additionally, there are flashcards and a bingo-type game.

> ➤ Fishing with Phonics
> ➤ Match of Mystery
> ➤ Storybook Reader
> ➤ Toon Book Reader

■ *Stage 1 Word Family Emergent Readers*
www.hubbardscupboard.org/printable_booklets.html#WordFamilyBooklets
Price: Free

Short stories with similar word families. Line drawings with simple sentences. People in drawings are children, but the nonfiction and some of the other stories are possibilities for older students.

■ *Florida Reading Research Student Center Activities*
(Florida Department of Education, 2005)
www.fcrr.org
Price: Free (online)

Phonological awareness and phonic activities made by Florida teachers. Each lesson has objectives, flashcards/game boards, etc., and directions for activities. This resource has hundreds of activities—almost too many—that can be downloaded and used immediately. The site may be hard to navigate, but it is worth the try. (I finally printed out all the activities so I could refer to them quickly.)

■ *Fun Fonix*
www.funfonix.com
Price: Free (online)

Worksheets, workbooks, simple clipart, and online phonics games.

■ *Printable flashcards*
www.mightyeducationsystems.com
Price: Free (online)

■ *ABC Fast Phonics* Price: Free (online)
www.abcfastphonics.com

ABC Fast Phonics, a website created by Carol Moore, uses fun cartoons and sounds with audio narration and clickable words to teach phonics. The program says it is good for both children and adults.

■ *Phonics for Free*
www.readingtarget.com
Price: Free

Worksheets and tests with cartoons that cover phonemic awareness and phonics rules.

- *Progressive Phonics* (all-in-one reading program)
  www.progressivephonics.com
  Price: Free (online)
     Phonics program with common sight words and handwriting practice. It also has activity sheets and flashcards.

Print Materials and Books

The instructional materials in this category are produced in print versions by traditional publishers. The costs range from nominal to very high. (Prices given here were current at the time of publication and are subject to change.)

- *Foundations: Word Families*
  The Wright Group (2000)
  Price: $180.08 for single copy of 30 books
  www.WrightGroup.com
     Foundations Word Family books can help students master early reading skills and recognize important word families and high-frequency words. The books are small sized with few pages and are probably only appropriate for elementary students. The words appear in the text and are also hidden in the illustrations so students can have fun finding them.

- *Bright Ideas for Growing Minds*
  Teach Bright (2005)
  www.teachbright.com
  Sorting Sounds— $21.99; Phonics Sorts—$21.99; Vocabulary Builders—$21.99;
  Sight Word Sentence Frames Level 1—$21.99;
  Sight Word Sentence Frames Level 2—$21.99; Sight Word Saver Set — $40.00
     Colorful photographs printed on ready-to-use punch-out cards and activities using the cards.

- *Early Phonics Readers*
  Continental Press
  Price: $3.25 per 8-page book
  www.continentalpress.com
  Long Vowel Books—12 books; Consonant Blends and Digraphs Books—12 books
     Suitable for elementary students only. Many pictures and stories are aimed at young children, but some are appropriate for older kids.

- **Chall-Popp Phonics**
  Continental Press
  Price: $12.95 for each of four levels of worksheets
  www.continentalpress.com
     Two sets of 12 books each. Drawings are usually appropriate for older readers, but characters are shown as children.

■ *Beginning Reading for Older Students*
Good Apple Publishing (2002)
Price: $12.95 (80 pages)
Available from online booksellers

Workbook-style book. Makes 30 small books that are adult-oriented with line drawings. Later books have graphic drawings like adult comics. Each book gets more complex in vocabulary and includes Dolch (common sight) words. The stories are not very interesting, but are very acceptable to older students.

■ *Readings for Older Students*
Remedia Publications
Price: $149.99 for 9 workbooks, software, and flashcards
www.rempub.com
  ➤ Phonics for Older Students
  ➤ Phonics Crossword Puzzles
  ➤ Phonics Word Search Puzzles
  ➤ Word Families for Older Students
  ➤ Sight Words for Older Students
  ➤ Basic Sight Words Flash Cards
  ➤ Basic Sight Words Software
  ➤ Quick Word Attack for Older Students
  ➤ E-Z Reading for Older Students

■ *Easy True Stories: A Picture-Based Beginning Reader (Sandra Heyer)*
Price: $24.95
Available from online booksellers

Twenty units each containing a picture vocabulary, a true life story adapted from a news or magazine article, and discussion questions. Student and teacher materials are included in one book. There are three more books in this series.

■ *Teaching Reading to Children with Down Syndrome (Patricia Oelwein)*
Woodbine House (1995)
Price: $24.95
www.woodbinehouse.com

This classic reading book, originally designed for children with Down syndrome, has been successfully used with students with other disabilities. The sight-word reading procedures can be adapted for older students by using pictures of older individuals.

■ *The PCI Reading Program*
PCI Education
Price: $630.00 for Level One (Reading books only, $74.95)
$1,979.95 for Level One, Level Two, and Three
www.pcieducation

The PCI Reading program is for nonreaders. It has much more repetition than other programs. Level One has almost 100 introductions of one word. In Level One, 140 basic sight and real-world words are taught through a system of repetition, hands-on practice, controlled-vocabulary books, evaluation materials, and other activities. Level

Two continues Level One activities and adds inflectional endings (/ed/, /ing/, etc.) and compound words. Level Three has word decoding through phonics, as well as instruction in comprehension, fluency, and writing.

■ *Action Reading Fundamentals*
Action Reading, Inc.
Price: $180
www.actionreading.com
  Eight audio CDs and a workbook make up this phonics reading program.

Smart Phones and Tablet Computer Apps

At the time of publication of this book, many apps are available to aid someone who is learning to read. However, depending on the companies making the phones or tablet computers, the apps available vary, depending on the specific type of phone or tablet computer you are using. You will need to preview the apps programs to see if they are age appropriate and address the content you wish to teach. Apps are often added or disappear in a short period of time. A sampling of apps available at the time this book was written is given below:

■ **Available from iKidApps (www.ikidapps.com):**
  ■ *Monkey and the Crocodile*
  Price: $0.99
    This interactive story tells a folk tale from India. The words can be read by the phone or computer as the story progresses.

  ■ *Wild Fables*
  Price: Free
    Aesop's fables told with student interaction on each page.

  ■ *The Cat In The Hat—Dr. SEUSS—Lite*
  Price: Free
    This story would be good for intermediate elementary students.

■ **Available from iTunes (www.apple.com/itunes):**
  ■ *Learning to Read*
  Price: $2.99
    This app is designed for learning vocabulary with pictures and pronunciation of the words following. It also includes Dolch sight words (most frequently used words that are not easily taught with pictures).

  ■ *Rock 'n Learn Phonics Easy Reader*
  Price: $1.99
    Three decodable stories teaching short vowels, consonant-vowel-consonant combinations, and words ending with ll, ss, ff, and s.

- *IBook*
  Price: Free
  > IBook makes it possible to download books from IBookstore. You need to know the name of the books that you want. The newest app has a read-aloud feature.

- *Word Wizard—Talking Moveable Alphabet and Spell Check*
  Price: $3.99
  > Teaches alphabet, making words, and spelling at various difficulty levels

- *Bob Books #1—Reading Magic*
  Price: $1.99
  > Phonics-based interactive games. Pictures may not be age-appropriate for older students.

- *PBS Kids videos*
  Price: Free
  > Videos from PBS programs, some on reading.

- **Other:**
  - *E-books for free for Kindle*
    www.amazon.com/Kindle
    > Volunteers have assembled these books that have text-speech capacity. They are often classics that are no longer under copyright protection. Therefore, they are mostly beyond the second grade reading level. You will have to determine the reading levels.

Computer Games and Programs

- *Bridge to Reading*
  www.yourchildlearns.com/bridge
  Price: Free
  > An interactive adventure tale in which the student types in a word and action occurs in the scene.

- *Learning A-Z*
  www.readinga-z.com
  Price $84.85
  > A complete reading program available online for a classroom of 1-9 students. Has phonics, sight words, and books at different levels.

- *Reading Is Fundamental: Reading Planet*
  http://www.rif.org/kids/readingplanet.htm
  Price: Free
  > Illustrated songs and stories read aloud by the computer, suitable for levels two and three in the Triangle approach.

References

Al Otaiba, S. & Hosp, M.K. (2004). Providing effective literacy instruction to students with Down syndrome. *Teaching Exceptional Children 36* (4), 28-35.

Allen, E. G. & Laminack, L. L (1982). Language experience reading—it's a natural. *Reading Teacher 35*(6), 708-714.

Allen, R.V. & Allen, C. (1982). Language Experience Activities. 2nd ed. Hopewell, NJ: Houghton Mifflin Company.

Ashton-Warner, S. (1986*). Teacher.* New York, NY: Touchstone/Simon & Schuster.

Biancarosa, C. & Snow, C. E. (2006). *Reading Next—A Vision for Action and Research in Middle and High School Literacy: A Report to Carnegie Corporation of New York.* 2nd ed. Washington, D.C.: Alliance for Excellent Education.

Browder, D., et al. (2006). Research on reading instruction for individuals with significant cognitive disabilities. *Exceptional Children 72*(4), 392-408.

Cole, K., Elliott, J., Estes, M., Goetze, J., Ferguson, P., and Marquez, D. (2002–2011). Starfall scope and sequence. Boulder, CO: Starfall Education.

Division of Research and Policy (2002*). Summary of the U.S. National Reading Panel Report Teaching Children to Read.* Newark, NJ: International Reading Association. www.nichd nih.gov/publications/pubskey.cfm?from=nrp

Dolch, E.W. (1948). Dolch word list in www.uniqueteachingresources.com/dolch-sight-words.

Elwell, C.E., Murray, R., & Kucia, M. M. (1988*). Phonics.* Cleveland: Modern Curriculum Press.

Engelmann, S. & Bruner, E. (1995). *Reading Mastery.* Chicago: Science Research Associates (SRA) /McGraw-Hill.

Engelmann, S., Hanner, S., and Johnson, G. (1999). *Corrective Reading Series Guide.* Columbus, OH: SRA/McGraw-Hill.

Fiester, L. (2010). *Early Warning! Why Reading by the End of Third Grade Matters.* Baltimore: Annie R. Casey Foundation.

Fountas, I. & Pinnell, G. (1999). *Matching Books to Readers: A Leveled Book List for Guided Reading.* Portsmouth, NH: Heinemann.

Fry, E. & Kress, J. *The Reading Teacher's Book of Lists.* 5th ed. San Francisco, CA: Jossey-Bass, 2006.

Gambell, M.A. & Sajtos, G.N. (2001). *An Individualized Computer-assisted Language Experience Remedial Reading Inquiry.* Saskatoon, Saskatchewan: McDowell Foundation for Research into Teaching.

Goodman, K.S. (2006). *What's Whole in Whole Language?* 2nd ed. New York, NY: Midpoint Trade Books.

Goodman, K. (1982). *Language and Literacy.* Boston, MA: Routledge & Kegan.

Hager, A. (2001). Techniques for teaching beginning-level reading to adults. *Focus on Basics* 5 (A). www.ncsall.net/?id=280.

Hall, M. (1978). The *Language Experience Approach for Teaching Reading: A Research Perspective.* 2nd ed. Newark, NJ: International Reading Association.

"High Frequency Words." Utah Education Network. www.uen.org/k-2educator/word_lists.shtml.

Hiebert, E. (1999). *Text Matters in Learning to Read.* (CIERA Report #1-1001). Ann Arbor, MI: University of Michigan School of Education, The Center for Improvement of Early Achievement.

Hildreth, G. (1965). Experience related reading for school beginners. *Elementary English 42:* 280-297.

Hold, G.M. (1995). Teaching low-level adult ESL learners. *ERIC Digest.* Washington, D.C.: ERIC Clearinghouse. www.ericdigests.org/1996-1/low.htm.

Kamil, M. (2003). *Adolescents and Literacy: Reading in the 21st Century.* Washington, DC: Alliance for Excellent Education.

Kendrick, W.M. (1966). A comparative study of two first grade language arts programs. *The Reading Teacher 20:* 25-30.

Lowrey, J.S. (1942, 2001). *The Poky Little Puppy.* New York, NY: Simon and Schuster.

Lyon, R.G. (2000). As quoted in Sherman, L., Why can't I read? *Northwest Education Magazine.* Portland, OR: Northwest Regional Educational Laboratory.

Lyon, R.G. (1999). Learning disabilities research. The Learning Disability Institute. www.ldinstitute.org/ Idieduresrch.shtml.

McCray, A.D., Vaughn, S., and Neal, L. I. (2001). Not all students learn to read by third grade: Middle school students speak out about their reading disabilities. *Journal of Special Education 35:* 17–30.

McShane, S. (2005). *Applying Research in Reading Instruction for Adults.* Washington, DC: National Institute for Literacy.

Murray, B. (2002). List of phonemes, spellings, and meaningful representations. [Hand gestures for phonemes]. The Reading Genie website. www.auburn.edu/academic/education/reading_genie.

National Institute of Child Health and Human Development. (2001). *Put Reading First: The Research Building Blocks for Teaching Children to Read.* Washington, DC: U.S. Government Printing Office.

The National Reading Panel Report. (2000). Teaching Children to Read: An Evidence-based Assessment of the Scientific Research Literature on Reading and Its Implications for Reading Instruction. Washington, DC: U.S. Government Printing Office (NIH Publication No. 00-4769).

Pierson, M. & Glaeser, B. (Spring 2003). Revisiting the language experience approach. *Academic Exchange Quarterly 7* (1): 122-4.

Quigley, S.P., McAnally, P.L, Rose, S., and King, C. M. (2001). *Reading Milestones.* 3rd ed. Austin, TX: Pro Ed.

Rog, L.J. & Burton, W. (2001). Matching the reader to the text: Leveling emergent reading materials for instruction and assessment. *The Reading Teacher 55* (4).

Sherman, L. (2003). Why can't I read? Current research offers new hope to disabled readers. *Northwest Education Magazine.*

Sing Your Way Through Phonics. Action Factor. www.actionfactor.com/pages/scope-and-sequence.html.

Stauffer, R. (1970). A language experience approach. In James Kerfoot, ed. *Perspectives in Reading, No. 5, First Grade Reading Programs.* Newark, NJ: International Reading Association.

Taylor, M. (1992). The language experience approach and adult learners. Center for Adult English Language Acquisition. www.cal.org/caela/esl_resources/digests/LEA.html.

Trammell, R. L. (Summer 1982). Why is it so hard to write a good R-controlled vowel rule? *Spelling Progress Bulletin:* 13-15. www.spellingsociety.org/bulletins/b82/summer/position3.php.

Vacca, J., Vacca, R., and Gove, M. (2000). *Reading and Learning to Read.* 4th ed. New York, NY: Longman.

Wise, J. & Buffington, S. (2005). *The Ordinary Parent's Guide to Teaching Reading.* Charles City, VA: Peace Hill Press.

Wren, S. & Watts, J. (2002). *The Abecedadrian Reading Assessment.* Austin, TX: Balanced Reading.

Index

About the Author

DeAnna Horstmeier has more than thirty years of experience as a special educator and consultant. She is a reading tutor and was formerly an Instructional Resources Consultant at a special education regional resource center in Columbus, Ohio, assisting parents and educators with teaching strategies and materials for their students. She also taught special education and speech, language, and communication at The Ohio State University. She is the author of *Teaching Math to People with Down Syndrome and Other Hands-On Learners, Books 1 & 2* (Woodbine House, 2004 & 2008).